T0065465

FINDING TRUTH

IN LIFE AND LOVE:

One Man's Journey

George Kyriacou

WESTBOW
PRESS®
A DIVISION OF THOMAS NELSON
& ZONDERVAN

This book is a work of non-fiction. Unless otherwise noted, the author and the publisher make no explicit guarantees as to the accuracy of the information contained in this book and in some cases, names of people and places have been altered to protect their privacy.

WestBow Press books may be ordered through booksellers or by contacting:

WestBow Press
A Division of Thomas Nelson & Zondervan
1663 Liberty Drive
Bloomington, IN 47403
www.westbowpress.com
844-714-3454

Scripture quotations marked NASB are taken from The New American Standard Bible®, Copyright © 1960, 1962, 1963, 1968, 1971, 1972, 1973, 1975, 1977, 1995 by The Lockman Foundation. Used by permission.

ISBN: 978-1-6642-5851-8 (sc)
ISBN: 978-1-6642-5850-1 (e)

Print information available on the last page.

WestBow Press rev. date: 04/08/2022

In loving memory of my mother, Eleni Kyriacou 1936-2018

But we remember you more than the laughs,
the big food and the big family.
It was your big love
That you taught us so unconditionally.

Poem by Theodosis Kyriacou
(Full poem at the back of this book)

Dedicated to and inspired by
My three beautiful daughters,
My one and only inspirational son,
And my amazing wife, my best friend and soul mate.
With eternal love.

Literary review by Dr. Lucy Edwards,
Elena Kyriacou and Zoe Georgiou
Book cover by Zoe Georgiou

CONTENTS

INTRODUCTION

*"The journey of a thousand miles begins with
a single step. Watch your step."*
Thomas S. Monson

*"The trouble with the rat race is that even
if you win, you're still a rat."*
Lily Tomlin

*"Life is a journey that must be travelled no matter
how bad the roads and accommodations."*
Oliver Goldsmith

"Finding Truth in Life and Love: One Man's Journey." Wow, what a title. I expect you are thinking the author is a renowned Nobel prize-winning scientist, an enlightened monk sitting on a mountain for decades meditating, or a crazed individual with delusions of grandeur. I hate to disappoint you, but I am none of these (well, maybe a little of the latter). I am, in some ways, a very ordinary person, living an ordinary life in an ordinary part of the world. I am also unique. No one else has my set of genes, my life experiences, my hurts, my triumphs. No one else has travelled the exact path I have trekked through life. At the very least, I am the only mortal that can explain my view of the world, which is very ordinary and extraordinary in equal measure.

Why write a book? Especially one with such wide-reaching claims? I have no expectations that this book will be next year's best-seller (or any other year's best-seller for that matter). Is it to become rich and famous? Very few authors become rich or famous, so why go to all the trouble to write a book? It is merely to explain my view of the world after carting my unique set of genes in this somewhat worn out, carbon-based body for the best part of sixty years in the hope that it will at least provoke a thought or two on the subjects at hand. At worst, I hope the reader will understand what makes me tick. The English language has never been my strong point, so I beg your understanding of my literary failings in the coming pages. I am sure if I had been schooled decades later, I would have been labelled dyslexic. When I was at school, people were not so understanding or kind. I do not think I was ever "officially" labelled as having learning difficulties or dyslexia, but I do remember being one of the only children taken out of the classroom and having one to one individual lessons with adults that were not part of the normal teaching staff. I think part of the reason for these sessions was because I was unable to spell my last name until quite late on in my primary education. I would sign my work George Ky. I remember feeling shame at this but also not putting in the effort to correct my shortcoming. It is only now in later life I wonder what these lessons where about. Isn't it funny what you remember?

Childhood: The early years

I was born in Cyprus, a small island in the eastern Mediterranean. I do not remember anything of the few months I spent on the island before my family and I immigrated to the United Kingdom. We moved primarily because my father was astute enough to foresee the invasion of Cyprus by the Turkish army. The invasion became a reality a decade later. My mother was always of a nervous disposition and had many phobias. My father knew that my mother struggled with the threat of war, let alone living through one. With this at the forefront of his mind, he decided to leave the country he loved for the sake of his family that he loved more. Over the years, I realised that I inherited my mother's phobias which were at times debilitating. I never really grew out of these fears until a lot later in life. The reason for getting over these hang-ups will become clear as the book unfolds.

I do consider myself a fortunate person. I was born in the '60s. The telephone was connected to the wall with a wire, and used for making telephone calls, hard to believe I know. You could not use the telephone to find out anything unless, of course, the person you called knew the answer. You learnt what your parents or teachers taught you. There were none of the distractions we have today. No personal music or other means of amusement. Interestingly the root of the word 'amuse' is French and means *"to divert the attention, beguile, delude."* Hard to believe, but that meant no constant bombardment of the mind through stimuli. Inevitably, this led to plenty of time to think and be alone with my thoughts. I wish the millennials could experience a moment of quiet reflection rather than the constant need to be plugged into the world via mobile phones and computers. This time of quiet reflection was both a blessing and a curse. A curse as my imagination would run wild, thinking that everyone's life was better than mine, but also a blessing, as I had the time to think about things outside of myself. I soon developed a keen sense of right and wrong. I was named the United Nations representative of the classroom, always wanting to resolve rather than retaliate.

In my early years, I always felt different because, well, I *was* different from my peers. The area my family and I initially settled in was a middle-class suburb of London. The only other ethnic minority child in the school was a Sikh boy. I can still picture his face but cannot for the life of me remember his name. We both felt distinctive because we were darker than the other kids and were teased for having hairy legs long before puberty. To compound my "special status," I started school not knowing a single word of English. A strange form of Greek, only spoken in Cyprus was my native language. I had never been far from my mother's apron strings, so my first day of school was stressful for all concerned. I screamed the house down, not wanting to leave home's familiarity for the strange alien world called school. My parents did what all parents do in these circumstances, they resorted to bribery. There were promises of sweets and toys. None of these seemed to reduce the flow of tears. Finally, in desperation, my parents told me that I could not be a doctor unless I went to school. The tears stemmed somewhat. After what seemed an eternity the school day was over, and I am sure the teachers were glad to see the back of the child that cried all day. I finally ran into my parents' arms and asked if I was now a doctor! They could not help but laugh. However, they were smart enough not to divulge how long it would take to become a doctor. I am not sure where the notion of being a physician came from. It certainly was not my idea!

I started working in the family fish and chip shop at the tender age of seven. The work was hard labour. I can vividly remember how grown up and elated I felt as my sisters and parents showed me how to prepare chips. As the days rolled into weeks and months, the thrill faded. It is hard to keep the motivation going, peeling potato after potato, month after month, year after year. My children always roll their eyes as I recall this story to them, much like I would have at their age if my elders told me a similar story. Working in the family business was not seen as unusual at the time. As a family, we only mixed with other Cypriots. This was because my parents worried about losing their culture and, frankly, could not communicate effectively in English so other Cypriots was the natural choice for social gatherings. All Cypriot children worked in their family's fish and chip shops. To this day, I do not understand why Cypriots ended up owning most fish and chip shops, selling the great British favourite and pretty much the only take away that was available in the '60s. Whilst other children were playing, I was working in the cold and wet making chips in some of my spare time.

As I mentioned before, there were no personal amusement systems. The Sony Walkman was a decade away, the home computer was two decades away, and smartphones three decades away. So, what to do with my thoughts while I was cold and damp peeling potatoes? Most of the time, I spent feeling sorry for myself, thinking that my parents were so cruel compared to the other kids at school. None of them had to work! The rest of the time I used my colourful imagination to think about surprisingly advanced subjects, like why some people suffer. Of course, I was thinking mostly about poor old me, peeling all those potatoes. Later in life, I would think back to these days and realise just how hard my parents worked for the family. Working in the family business was what was expected of my siblings and me. That was just what we did. Cypriot families helped each other, but the culture around me was quite different. This led to my feeling sorry for myself rather than being grateful for having such caring and industrious parents. The sense of hard work rubbed off on my sisters and I and served us well in later life. I am so grateful to my parents for the work ethic they imparted in us at such a young age.

My family moved from a relatively affluent suburb of London to a deprived inner-city borough. The beautiful parklands made way to factories and houses that rarely had a garden of any significant size. The move was a real culture shock to my family and me. We moved from an area where there were just a few children from overseas, to a school where children from distant lands were in the majority. I remember my first day at my new primary school, to say it was a rough school is an understatement. I ended up being involved in several fights! It was all about pecking order in this school. Apparently, I looked "tough," so the other children needed to ascertain just how tough I was by picking a fight with me. Once they saw me repeatedly crying, the other children quickly realised I was no threat and left me alone. I became miserable and began comfort eating, quickly piling on the kilos, which further led to more teasing and bullying at school, which then led to more comfort eating. A vicious circle of events that is all too often repeated amongst the adolescent.

Starting secondary school, things were worse still. It was a massive comprehensive school with over 300 children per year group. The school had over 2000 children in total. It was so notorious for bad behaviour that the bus drivers refused to pick up the students from school as they feared for their safety, and for good reason I may add. Fights would break out between the students at rival schools. My friends, some of the better-behaved children, frequently shoplifted from the local sweetshops and played truant. I would be teased as a "goody-two-shoes" for not participating in these activities. As I mentioned earlier, I had a keen sense of wrong and right and copying my peers did not sit well with me. And so, the teasing continued even by my "friends." The comfort eating, along with the weight gain, continued to the point that I was one of the last to be picked for any team sports at school. It was humiliating.

My family and I went on three holidays to Cyprus during my childhood. The first time was in 1970. The experience was a real eye opener. Cyprus had not long been granted independence from Britain. As a young nation, Cyprus was decades behind Britain in terms of development. Using mules and donkeys as a form of transport and beasts of burden were still commonplace on the island. A third of all Cypriots gained employment in family-run farms as agriculture was by far the most significant source of employment. As a hot country, a farmer's life was a harsh occupation. The lack of rain meant that crops would need irrigating artificially using windmills, and for the more affluent farmers, diesel engines would pump water out of the ground from underwater springs to irrigate the crops. My family came from a small village in the Famagusta district of Cyprus, this area was known for producing distinctive Cyprus potatoes. The unique flavour of these potatoes is attributed to the red soil that was commonplace in this part of the island.

Like most youngsters, I was addicted to watching television. However, in Cyprus, the one state-owned television station would not start broadcasting until the early evening and finish around midnight. With the lack of broadcast entertainment, my extended family spent much of their time entertaining themselves. Hospitality was high on every Cypriots agenda. You could not go to a relative's home without being offered food and drink. It was almost an insult if you left without eating and drinking something. When Cypriots were not entertaining or working, it was common for the menfolk to go to the coffee shop to catch up on the latest gossip, play cards or backgammon. The exaggerated throwing of dice and slapping of the plastic pieces on the wooden board would echo around the coffee shop. Politics, a national pastime in Cyprus, invaded even this leisure activity. There would be a coffee shop for the left and right-wing political parties. Even locally produced drinks had left or right-wing associations, and so you would only order drinks linked with your political leanings. These extreme political views have led to fanaticism and many a family feud.

The women folk would gather in each other's homes for a Greek coffee and catch up with the latest gossip, usually while crocheting or knitting. Doing nothing was just not an option. Cypriot women were always doing something for fear of being branded a bad woman. Laziness meant single girls would struggle to find a good husband,

and married women had the family reputation to consider. Looking back in time, what these women complained about would not be regarded as worthy of repeating in today's world. I remember one conversation where one of my relatives said that her neighbour must have been a terrible wife because she let her husband put out the washing to dry on the clothesline. It was a real scandal and the talk of the village. Somehow the neighbour's actions would surely mean she was an immoral woman according to the gossip. How the world has changed.

In 1974, our family life took a further turn of fortunes. My father's prediction of the invasion of Cyprus became a reality with devastating consequences. Several family members lost their lives in the fierce fighting that followed, including my mother's first cousin. He was studying to be a doctor in Greece. As his bad fortune would have it, he was in Cyprus for the summer to see his parents when he was called up for active duty. Unfortunately, he was never seen alive again. Even though the fighting was raging 2000 miles away, we felt the effects at home in Britain. My mother would listen to the radio for hours for news of the conflict in Cyprus. She would cry incessantly for her family. Almost all of our extended family had lost their homes and were now refugees in their own country. Their misery was compounded as our village was just the other side of no man's land. The family could almost touch their homes but were prevented from returning by thousands of Turkish soldiers.

We lived in a two-bedroom flat above the fish and chip shop my parents owned. The flat was cramped for the five members of the family at the best of times. We then housed several relatives that had lost their homes during the invasion and were now refugees. I used to sleep on the passage floor with my cousin. The inhabitants of this small flat had long occupied all the bedrooms, and so the passage floor sufficed as a makeshift bedroom. The apartment was bulging at the seams. As you can imagine, there was no privacy to be had. Even using the bathroom would come with an urgent tap on the door as someone needed to use these most precious of facilities.

I remember going to my first funeral as a young teenager. The widow was whaling at the top of her voice as they lowered her deceased husband into the ground. She was so grief-stricken that she tried to get into the grave with him to everyone's horror. It was a harrowing experience for my sisters and I. I was so traumatised by the experience that I could not attend funerals until way into my adult life. However, the incident did waken some latent thoughts about what life is all about. Is life just this brief period we spend on earth, or is there an afterlife? All major religions seem to major on something happening after this earthly existence. Was an afterlife just wishful thinking for those facing the loss of a loved one rather than facing up to our mortality?

I was brought up a nominal Christian, going to a Greek Orthodox Church on a Sunday (kicking and screaming mostly). I had a very vague understanding of Christianity, but my first biology lesson at secondary school on evolution confused me. It stated that life evolved to what we see today without the need for divine intervention. Christianity and evolution seemed to crash into each other. Even at this tender age, I suspected that these two competing ideas could not co-exist. I deduced that one was wrong and the other right at best, or at worst, both notions were wrong. One thing was for sure they could not both be right because of the clashing claims. I was convinced that science-based evolution had to be right and Christianity wrong. Christianity was based on old ideas and some strange Jewish character called Jesus, who seemed to think it was necessary to get himself killed. Besides, if Christianity were proven wrong, there would no longer be a need to go to church. Why was I a Christian anyway? It seems that if I had been born into a Muslim home, I would have been a Muslim, and if I were born in a Sikh family, I would have been a Sikh. The religion a person is born into does not seem to be a good reason to believe in that faith system. In any case, why were there so many religions? It seemed that they could not all be true, as they made bold and contrary claims. Therefore, at best only one religion could be true, and at worse, none were true.

In hindsight, I wanted evolution, and by extension, atheism to be right so I could get out of going to church. In Orthodox Christianity, the service goes on for hours and is performed in a form of Greek that I could not understand. Without making a conscious decision, I embarked on a journey for truth that would span half a century.

Truth

What is truth? The Colins English dictionary defines truth as: - *"Truth, the quality of true, genuine, actual, or factual. A proven or verified fact, principle, etc."* In today's world, it seems that the word truth has been transformed to mean what an individual wants to believe rather than a reflection of reality. In 2016, the Oxford dictionary international word of the year was "post-truth", after the acrimonious US presidential election, and the BREXIT referendum caused a stellar increase in the word's usage. Post-truth is defined as *"objective facts are less influential in shaping public opinion than appeals to emotion and personal belief."* Again, this was highlighted in the 2020 US election, where the loser claimed foul play in the election process without providing a shred of evidence to substantiate these claims. Deadly consequences ensued as his followers went on a rampage. It seems that the one thing I have been looking to find, the truth is now not as important as a person's emotions. How did this happen? Why are people more concerned with their feelings than the truth? Steve Turners satirical poem, *"Creed,"* describes the modern mind beautifully. Below are the last few sentences, but I recommend reading it in full.

> *We believe that each man must find the truth*
> *that is right for him.*
> *Reality will adapt accordingly.*
> *The universe will readjust. History will alter.*
> *We believe that there is no absolute truth*
> *excepting the truth that there is no absolute truth.*

Is the last sentence of the poem true? *"We believe that there is no absolute truth excepting the truth that there is no absolute truth."* I was determined not to be drawn into today's narrative and plunge ahead for the truth. To be true to the Socratic principle, which is to *"follow the argument wherever it leads."*

The first stop was to evaluate Evolution and Darwinism. Charles Robert Darwin was an English Biologist known as the father of evolution, his proposition that all species of life have descended from simple common ancestors is considered a fundamental concept in science. If Darwin was right and man evolved from simple creatures without divine intervention, then there was no need for a creator and by extension attending those long church services.

CHAPTER 1
SCIENCE

"Science is organized knowledge. Wisdom is organized life."
Immanuel Kant

*"We live in a society exquisitely dependent on science
and technology, in which hardly anyone knows
anything about science and technology."*
Carl Sagan

*"The saddest aspect of life right now is that science gathers
knowledge faster than society gathers wisdom."*
Isaac Asimov

Darwinism

As a child, my family and I loved watching wildlife programmes on television. My mother, being a typical Cypriot, would wonder what species of wildlife were edible. She would cry out it was a shame when a predator would make a meal of a deer or something else that mum would consider particularly tasty. Watching one of these wildlife programmes, I remember David Attenborough explaining how giraffes got their long neck. Attenborough contended that it was the competition for leaves on trees that had led to the evolution of the animal's long neck. I was just a young kid at the time, but this did seem very odd. How could competition change an organism's physical attributes? It is not just a case of developing a long neck; it would mean that the giraffe would need to have a big heart to generate enough blood pressure to reach its brain. When the animal bends down to drink water, it needs a mechanism to stop blood rushing to its brain, causing the animal to blackout. The whole concept of evolution seemed bizarre to me, but Darwinism and evolution I was told was an established science. Besides, who was I to dispute our national treasure, David Attenborough.

Later in life, I started reading and listening to alternative views on evolution, notably Dr A. E. Wilder-Smith in his books, for example, *"The Natural Sciences Know Nothing of Evolution."* Wilder-Smith must be one of the most intelligent men I have ever had the privilege to read. He has three earned doctorates. First, he obtained a Ph. D. in physical organic chemistry in his twenties. The second doctorate was gained in pharmacology and a third in pharmacological sciences. While his books can be heavy going, Wilder-Smith's primary argument against evolution is the genetic code's complexity. The genetic code is the most complicated code known to man. If you unravelled the DNA in one person you could stretch it to Pluto and back. DNA is such an incredibly efficient storage system that engineers are actively trying to work out ways of using DNA as a means of storing data for use in computer science. How could this code have evolved by chance? No other known code is formed by chance. In fact, it is the removal of chance elements that codes rely on to convey a message. We have many software coders at my place of work. If I told them that we would no longer require their services because the code they write would occur "spontaneously," they would be horrified and probably sit me down on the nearest psychiatrist's couch for "a chat." Wilder-Smith explains that the materialist formula for life is energy plus matter plus time is deficient. It leaves out the need for information entirely, such as the information that is found in the genetic code. Microbiology has also shown how "simple cell" organisms are anything but simple. These organisms are tiny microbiological machines doing incredible work to sustain life. Simple cell organisms have tiny "motors" that help them move and other teleonomic (purposeful) functions. These "motors" revolve at 100,000 revolutions per minute. John Von Neumann, the famous Hungarian American Mathematician said, *"Every living cell is a machine, supremely complex, capable of reproduction, growth, survival, self-diagnosing, self-repairing, with a complex cellular communication of information storage retrieval and application."*

The more I researched Darwinism, the more I realised the lack of evidence for the theory. I was not alone in my opinions. The groundswell of scientists coming to the same conclusion was increasing. Scientist like Stephen Meyer, David Berlinski and Michael Behe to name a few. If Darwinism is a scientific fact, we should see the evidence in the geological records. For example, why are there not all the different length of giraffe's necks found in the fossil record? David Berlinski says, *"There are gaps in the fossil graveyard, places where there should be intermediate forms, but where there is nothing whatsoever instead. No palaeontologist denies that this is so. It is simply a fact; Darwin's theory and the fossil record are in conflict."* Stephen Meyers book, *"Darwin's Doubt,"* expands on this at great length.

What is even more disturbing is a vast amount of "evidence"

for evolution has been disproven or fabricated. To falsify evidence is particularly worrying. Why would a scientist do this? An example of these hoaxes is Piltdown man. Piltdown man was supposed to be the missing evolutionary link between apes and man. Charles Dawson, an amateur archaeologist, verified its antiquity and pronounced that it was part of a skull that was possibly human. Dawson began to search for the rest of the skull. In 1912, a jawbone was discovered. Dawson and palaeontologist Arthur Woodward verified that the skull had human features and the jaw was ape-like. The fossils became known as Piltdown Man. At last, scientists believed that here was "proof" that apes had evolved into humans! However, in 1953, Piltdown man was exposed as a forgery. It was discovered that the skull was from a modern human and that the jawbone and teeth were from an orangutan. The teeth were filed down in an attempt to make them look human. The bones and teeth were chemically treated to give them the appearance of being ancient. This is just one example of fabricated "evidence" for evolution.

I believe that Darwinism has racist undertones. Darwin's book full name is *"On the Origin of Species by Means of Natural Selection, or the Preservation of Favoured Races in the Struggle for Life."* Who are the *"Favoured Races?"* The Nazis believed that the Jewish race was inferior, and the Aryan race was "favoured." The Nazis thought evolution would eventually render the Jews extinct. During the Second World War, the Nazis embarked on the Holocaust, which was industrialising the Jewish race's annihilation. The Nazis were "helping" speed up what they thought was an inevitable evolutionary process.

In conclusion, there seems to be no evidence of macroevolution, that is, large-scale evolution involving new organisms' appearance. In short, dogs remain dogs, and cats remain cats. That is not to say that microevolution does not occur, which is small evolutionary changes over a short time. For example, you can breed dogs to have different coloured coats or other features. These are provable and repeatable and backed up by the science of genetics thanks to the work of Gregor Mendel, the Augustinian monk. Mendel's paper, published in 1866, spelt out the principles of genetics and is still current. Through his work on pea plants, Mendel discovered that genes (a unit of heredity) come in pairs and are inherited from each of the parents. Mendel's research led him to conclude that genes will influence the offspring's appearance depending on the dominant or recessive gene traits. Furthermore, Mendel realised that there was a mathematical pattern that could predict the characteristics of the offspring. On the other hand, Darwin's theory of evolution is just that, a theory. Like all scientific theories, it is open to being superseded when better research becomes available or if more plausible theories are proposed. Evolution also flies in the face of the second law of thermodynamics. In layman's terms, the law of thermodynamics states that everything is tending towards chaos. All other branches of science embrace this law except evolution which suggests organisms are becoming more complex. Darwin himself had doubts about elements of his theory. He wrote to his friend Dr Joseph Hooker, *"The rapid development as far as we can judge of all the higher plants within recent geological times is an abominable mystery."* A famous Chinese palaeontologist Jun-Yuan Chen, whose latest discoveries seem to add further doubts to Darwin's theories, was cautioned by a reporter who thought his views would get him in trouble with his government. Jun-Yuan Chen said, *"In China we can criticise Darwin, but not the government; in America, you can criticise the government, but not Darwin."* Somewhat humorously, this points to the almost reverent belief some have in a theory with little evidential basis.

It seems that many biologists acknowledge the weakness of Darwin's theory, and many new theories have been postulated to explain how life has continuously evolved into the creatures that we see in the world today. None of these theories has gathered enough evidence to transition from a scientific theory to a scientific fact. Furthermore, Darwin's theory does not explain how life started in the first place. Science has lots of theories but no firm proof on how life started on earth.

What does this mean for my quest for truth? While I am by no means an expert on Darwin or evolution, I believe that it draws a line under the evolution of simple to complex creatures being explained by Darwinism or any other currently known science. What conclusions should I draw from this? Is intelligent design, which is code for theism (belief in God), the only possible explanation? What if it is simply that biology has not come up with the answers so far but will do in the future? I concluded that this was a possibility and so shelved how life started on Earth and looked to the universe's origins. Maybe I would have more luck here to prove that science could explain how the universe came into existence.

Origins of the Universe

Darwinism has not been able to explain the origins of life or how complex creatures evolve from simple organisms. The more I studied evolution, the more persuaded I am that this is not a plausible explanation for how life on earth evolved. Would an attempt to understand the origins of the universe be more conclusive using current scientific methods? Is there a scientific explanation as to how the earth on which we live came into existence? Clearly you need an earth in the first place for life to thrive on. Is there truth in the current scientific theories on the universe origins? It is cosmology's most fundamental question: How did the universe begin?

The first fact to note is the universe did indeed have a beginning. Before 1929, many scientists circumnavigated the question of the universe's origin, postulating that the cosmos always existed. If this were true, there would be no need to explain how the universe came to exist. Why there is something rather than nothing? A perpetual universe seemed a reasonable explanation until 1929, Edwin Hubble noticed that most galaxies were moving away from the Earth, indicating an expanding universe. The logical conclusion is that the universe expanded from a central point. Various theories have been proposed to explain the cause of the expanding universe.

The most popular hypothesis to explain origins is the Big Bang theory. George Lemaitre, a Belgian astronomer and Catholic priest, proposed the Big Bang Theory in the 1920's. The theory states that the universe as we know it started with a small singularity, then inflated violently some 13.8 billion years ago to the cosmos that we know today. This fitted perfectly with Hubble's discovery of an expanding universe a few years later. Current instruments do not allow astronomers to peer back at the universe's birth. Much of what we understand about the Big Bang Theory comes from mathematical formulas and models. Other theories to explain the origins of the universe exist. For example, in early 2020, the media was awash with reports that the New Horizons spacecraft had "decisively" overturned the Big Bang Theory. The new discovery seemed to suggest the gentle accumulation of matter to form the universe as opposed to the violent expanding universe previously postulated. There are yet other theories, such as eternal inflation or an oscillating universe. There seems to be an endless list of ideas to explain how the universe was set in motion. What all these theories on origins tend to have in common is the need for an old cosmos. Is there evidence of an old earth and universe? No one can be sure how old the universe is. After all, no one was there, meaning there is no historical evidence. No scientific method can "*prove*" the age of the universe. The calculated age of the universe make assumptions about past events, an example being the starting time of the 'clock'. The clock's speed and that the clock was never disturbed. None of this can science prove conclusively. Armed with the need for an old universe to explain current theories, is there evidence of an old cosmos? Below are some examples that seem to show the Earth is not billions of years old.

- Comets are essentially giant snowballs flying through space. Fragments of the comet "fall off" as it hurls through space. The elements that break off form the comet trails that we can observe. The most famous of all comets is Hailie's Comet. Scientists have calculated that the comet's disintegration rate means that comets can only be around 10,000 years old. Today we still see comets which means either comets are still being produced, comets are only a recent phenomenon, or the universe is less than 10,000 years old.

- Blood and soft tissue have been found in dinosaur fossils. Scientists struggle to explain how this is possible if dinosaurs fossils are hundreds of millions of years old.

- Every year water and wind erode about 20 billion tons of dirt and rock debris. If the Earth were billions of years old, it would make sense that there would be a lot more soil on the seabed.

- The Earth is surrounded by a magnetic field that protects life on Earth from solar radiation. Without this protective umbrella, life on Earth would not be sustainable. Scientists were surprised to discover that the field is quickly wearing down. However, at the current decay rate, the field and so the Earth could be no older than 20,000 years old.

- During the radioactive decay of uranium and thorium contained in rocks, helium is produced. Because helium is the second lightest element and a noble gas, it does not combine with other atoms—it readily diffuses (leaks) out and eventually escapes into the atmosphere. Helium diffuses so rapidly that all the helium should have leaked out in less than 100,000 years. So why are these rocks still full of helium atoms?

- Carbon-14 (or radiocarbon) is a radioactive form of carbon that scientists use to date fossils. But it decays so quickly, with a half-life of only 5,730 years, none is expected to remain in fossils after only a few hundred thousand years.

Yet carbon-14 has been detected in "ancient" fossils, which are supposedly hundreds of millions of years old.

As we understand more about the universe, the universe's fine-tuning seems to be incredibly well balanced. The late Stephen Hawking said, *"The laws of science, as we know them at present, contain many fundamental numbers, like the size of the electric charge of the electron and the ratio of the masses of the proton and the electron.... The remarkable fact is that the values of these numbers seem to have been finely adjusted to make possible the development of life."* Some scientists have called this "The Goldilocks syndrome." That is, the Earth's properties are precisely right for sustaining life. A few examples of this fine-tuning are as follows: -

- The Earth is exactly the right distance from the sun. If the Earth were further away, we would all freeze. If any closer, we would all burn up.
- The size of the Earth is precisely right to hold the correct proportions of nitrogen and oxygen. If the Earth were smaller, an atmosphere would be impossible. Any bigger its atmosphere would contain free hydrogen-like Jupiter. The Earth is the only planet known to science to have life.
- The moon is the exact size and distance from the Earth to enable tides to ensure the Earth's waters do not stagnate by causing tides.

These apparent fine-tuned examples have led some scientists like Freeman Dyson to say, *"The more evidence I find that the universe in some sense knew we were coming."* The laws of nature seem to have been crafted and fine-tuned to sustain life.

To overcome the problem of apparent design from a fine-tuned universe, some scientists propose a multiverse theory. The multiverse theory states that there are multitudes of universes, each formed entirely randomly, with our universe being the only one (or one of a few) that randomly developed in such a way that it supports life. This theory means the chances of having a universe capable of sustaining life, like ours, more likely. Cosmologist Edward Harrison says, *"Take your choice: blind chance that requires multitudes of universes, or design that requires only one."* Philosopher Richard Swinburne says, *"To postulate a trillion-trillion other universes, rather than one God, in order to explain the orderliness of our universe, seems the height of irrationality."* Finally, the multiverse hypothesis proves nothing, in that it does not answer how or why any universe came into existence.

After my admittedly superficial look at the origins of the universe, it seems that there are multiple theories but no conclusive facts on how the universe came to be. It is surprising that in the 21st century, we still know so little about how life and the universe started.

CHAPTER 2
THEISM

"When the missionaries came to Africa they had the Bible and we had the land. They said 'Let us pray.' We closed our eyes. When we opened them we had the Bible and they had the land."
Desmond Tutu

"Religion is what keeps the poor from murdering the rich."
Napoleon Bonaparte

"Not only does God play dice, but... he sometimes throws them where they cannot be seen."
Stephen Hawking

Is Theism true?

To my surprise, science has been unable to prove the origins of life or the universe. It seems that we, as humans, are none the wiser about how we got here despite all the hype of scientific progress. There are countless theories to explain origins but no conclusive proof. There is a reason for so many competing theories. All have weaknesses in their argument, and so a plethora of theories are postulated. Could this mean that scientific discoveries have not yet uncovered these secrets, but given time, will one day? I decided to pursue my quest for truth from a different position. If I could prove that a theistic answer was not possible, then by a process of elimination, it would mean that a naturalistic explanation must exist, all be it elusive for now. In the final analysis, there are only two possibilities. Either there is a God (or gods) that created everything, or there is not. Either man invented god or God invented man. I was sure that proving God's nonexistence would be an easy task.

Where do I start on my task to disprove the existence of God? There seem to be so many gods to explore. Each culture and race seem to have its deity that they cling to. Do all these (or some of these gods) exist? Are they all in heaven, fighting for the affections of humanity? I have heard many people say that all religions are fundamentally the same but superficially different. Is this true? While I am not an expert on world religion, I know that Buddhists do not believe in god. Hindus believe in a plethora of gods. Do I explore all these possibilities and eliminate them one by one? Looking closely at the major religions, far from being fundamentally the same but superficially different, they all seem to claim exclusivity. That is, their way is the only way. Logic dictates two mutually exclusive truth claims cannot both be right, so logically speaking, either all religions are false or at best, only one can be right.

I decided to start by investigating Christianity. The two most prominent world religions, Christianity, and Islam recognise Jesus as an essential part of their respective faiths. Christians regard Jesus as the Messiah, the fulfilment of Jewish prophecies and the saviour of humankind. Islam believes that Jesus was a prophet, just not divine. That made it easy. Look into the historical Jesus, which should go a long way to solve the theism's conundrum. Who was Jesus? Did he exist? Was he just a wise man? Was he God and rose from the dead? One thing is certain, no other person in history has had so much written about them. Jesus inspired Napoleon to say, *"Alexander, Caesar, Charlemagne, and I have founded empires. But on what did we rest the creations of our genius? Upon force. Jesus Christ founded his empire upon love; and at this hour millions of men would die for him."* The Bible is also the world's bestselling book year after year. It seemed that these facts alone would make this a worthwhile endeavour. The first step would be to discover what other non-Biblical ancient manuscripts have to say about Jesus, or is He only mentioned in the Bible? It would seem reasonable that if Jesus did exist, other historical writings would mention such an important personality that has spawned the world's biggest religion as well as inspiring more writings, art and music than any other person in history.

Nonbiblical evidence of Jesus' existence

My research revealed that there are several ancient non-biblical references to Jesus and Christians. The below is a small summary of some of these.

Tacitus (56-120 AD)

Cornelius Tacitus was a senator under Emperor Vespasian and was also a proconsul of Asia and he was a well-respected historian. In one of his most famous works, the *"Annals"* of 116 AD, which covered the period of Augustus' death in 14 AD to the death of Nero in 68 AD. Tacitus describes Emperor Nero's response to Rome's great fire and Nero's claim that the Christians were to blame.

"Consequently, to get rid of the report, Nero fastened the guilt and inflicted the most exquisite tortures on a class hated for their abominations, called Christians by the populace. Christus, from whom the name had its origin, suffered the extreme penalty during the reign of Tiberius at the hands of one of our procurators, Pontius Pilatus, and a most mischievous superstition, thus checked for the moment, again broke out not only in Judea, the first source of the evil, but even in Rome, where all things hideous and shameful from every part of the world find their centre and become popular. Accordingly, an arrest was first made of all [Christians] who pleaded guilty; then, upon their information, an immense multitude was convicted, not so much of the crime of firing the city, as of hatred against mankind. Mockery of every sort was added to their deaths. Covered with the skins of beasts, they were torn by dogs and perished, or were nailed to crosses, or were doomed to the flames and burnt, to serve as a nightly illumination, when daylight had expired."

What do we learn about Jesus from Tacitus? Jesus is referred to here as the Christus, a common miss-spelling of Christ. Pontius Pilate had Jesus killed; Tiberius was Emperor of Rome at the time. Jesus lived in Judea, and his followers were called Christians. The "mischievous superstition" alludes to Jesus' resurrection. Tacitus writings confirm the spread of Christianity from Judea to Rome.

Pliny the Younger (61-113 AD)

Pliny the Younger was the governor of the Roman province of Bithynia, located in Asia Minor. In the year 112 AD, in a letter to the Roman emperor Trajan, he describes early Christians' lifestyles.

"They were in the habit of meeting on a certain fixed day before it was light, when they sang in alternate verses a hymn to Christ, as to a god, and bound themselves by a solemn oath, not to any wicked deeds, but never to commit any fraud, theft or adultery, never to falsify their word, nor deny a trust when they should be called upon to deliver it up; after which it was their custom to separate, and then reassemble to partake of food—but food of an ordinary and innocent kind."

What do we learn about Jesus and Christians from Pliny the Younger? Christians believe that Christ is God. Christ's followers believed in an upright, moral lifestyle by abstaining from committing adultery, lying, stealing and generally maintaining high moral standards. Christians meet on a "fixed-day," which is the Sabbath.

Mara Bar-Serapion (70 AD)

Mara Bar-Serapion was a Syrian philosopher. In a letter to his son, he highlights the persecution of three wise men, Socrates, Pythagoras and a wise Jewish king, thought to be Jesus. The fact that Jesus is compared with other known philosophers of the ancient world shows that Jesus was an influential historical figure.

"What benefit did the Athenians obtain by putting Socrates to death? Famine and plague came upon them as judgment for their crime. Or, the people of Samos for burning Pythagoras? In one moment, their country was covered with sand. Or the Jews by murdering their wise king? After that their kingdom was abolished. God rightly avenged these men...The wise king...Lived on in the teachings he enacted."

What do we learn about Jesus from Mara Bar-Serapion? Jesus died because of the Jews. Jesus was a "wise man." The Jews suffered after the death of Jesus, referring to Rome's persecution of the Jews after the revolt in (66 AD) and destruction of the temple in (70 AD). Jesus' teachings lived on after his death.

Lucian of Samosata (115-200 AD).

Lucian was a satirist who was sarcastic about Christ and Christians. In his sarcasm, he did inadvertently acknowledge Christians and their belief in the crucified Jesus.

"The Christians, you know, worship a man to this day—the distinguished personage who introduced their novel rites, and was crucified on that account....You see, these misguided creatures start with the general conviction that they are immortal for all time, which explains the contempt of death and voluntary self-devotion which are

so common among them; and then it was impressed on them by their original lawgiver that they are all brothers, from the moment that they are converted, and deny the gods of Greece, and worship the crucified sage, and live after his laws. All this they take quite on faith, with the result that they despise all worldly goods alike, regarding them merely as common property." (Lucian, The Death of Peregrine. 11-13)

What do we learn about Jesus from Lucian? Jesus was crucified, that Christians believe in a life after death, so they did not fear death. They were monotheistic, did not attach importance to worldly goods, followed the teachings of Jesus, and considered a common bond between all Christians.

Alexamenos-Graffito (approximately 200 AD)

It is not commonly known that graffiti is not a modern form of expression. People have been leaving their marks on walls for thousands of years. The Alexamenos Graffito is believed to date from around 200 AD. It is possibly the earliest surviving depiction of Jesus. It shows Jesus in an unflattering light. As well as being one of the earliest depictions of Jesus, it may also be one of the earliest images of the Crucifixion. The cross was not seen as an emblem of Christianity until a lot later in history. The Crucifixion was rarely featured in Christian art before the 6th century. The so-called Alexamenos graffito represents a satirical representation of Christian worship. The drawing, scratched crudely into the soft plaster, shows a man worshipping a figure on a cross with the head of a donkey. There is an inscription in Greek, which translates roughly to *"Alexamenos worships his god,"* The artist of the graffiti mocks both Jesus and Alexamenos (a Christian) at the same time.

What do we learn from Alexamenos-Graffito? Christians believed their God (Jesus) was crucified on the cross. Non-Christians openly mocked Christians—a common theme in the early church.

Evidence for Jesus existence

As the previous pages testify, there is considerable non-biblical evidence for the existence of Jesus. The non-biblical accounts of Jesus cohere with elements of the Bible. These historical records indicate that Jesus was crucified under Pontius Pilot, a Roman procurator in Judea, while Emperor Tiberius reined. Pilot crucified Jesus to appease the demands of the Jews. Jesus' life (and death) spawned a new religion called Christianity. Jesus followers were willing to die for their newfound beliefs. Of all the New Testament events, the early Christians' willingness to die for their faith were crucial in this new religion. Why would these early Christians be prepared to die for their beliefs? It can only be that they believed in their convictions. They would surely only voluntarily die for what they perceived to be true. The question is, was what they believed factual? How could I determine this? I would need to examine the Bible to see what was taught, was it worth dying for, and lastly and most importantly, is the Bible true or have all Christian martyrs died for a false belief?

I had previously read the Bible periodically and found some parts inspiring, for example, the Sermon on the Mount. These ideals seemed like an excellent way for people to live but was it just that, a moral code? There are many such moral codes; what would make the Bible different is if it had a transcendent authority behind it. Were the words penned in the Bible inspired by man or God? Understanding my limitations in ascertaining the truth, I enlisted the assistance of an investigative journalist, Lee Strobel, by reading his book "The Case for Christ." Lee was an atheist, but his investigations into the Bible convinced him that the case for Christianity was overwhelming. He said, *"In short, I didn't become a Christian because God promised I would have an even happier life than I had as an atheist. He never promised any such thing. Indeed, following him would inevitably bring divine demotions in the eyes of the world. Rather, I became a Christian because the evidence was so compelling that Jesus really is the one-and-only Son of God who proved his divinity by rising from the dead. That meant following him was the most rational and logical step I could possibly take.*"

Lee's views seemed compelling, but I wanted to see if others had come to the same conclusion based on evidence alone and not on Christianity's pre-conceived ideas. I started to read the views of Jim Warner Wallace in his book *"Cold case Christianity."* Jim was also an atheist like Lee. Jim started reading the Bible because he was sure his skills as a cold case detective would prove that Christianity's claims would be false. Cold case detectives investigate historical unsolved murder cases where there are no eyewitnesses or forensic evidence and try to solve them. Jim concluded to his surprise (and mine) that Christianity was true based on evidence alone.

Jim's arguments were very well-reasoned and made sense. However, both Jim Wallace and Lee Strobel were atheist. Could it be that atheists were particularly biased, wanting to believe in something rather than nothing? How would another non-Christian theist fare, investigating the Bible? Surely someone who had strong convictions in another faith would not be swayed into believing in Christianity. In his book, *"Seeking Allah finding Jesus,"* Nabeel Qureshi describes how as a follower of Islam, he debated many Christians on the truth claims of the Bible. Finally, Nabeel was persuaded that Christianity was true and that becoming a Christian was the only option left open to him, considering the facts alone. Nabeel's conversion cost him his fellowship with his family, who he loved dearly. He did not make the decision to convert to Christianity lightly but based on what he believed to be overwhelming evidence. Nabeel said, *"After studying the historical origins of the Christian faith, I came to these conclusions: that Jesus died on the cross is as certain as anything historical can be; that he rose from the dead is by far the best explanation of the events surrounding his death; and that Jesus claimed to be God is the best explanation for the immediate Christian proclamation of Jesus' deity. Putting it all together: Jesus claimed to be God, and he proved it by rising from the dead. The case for Christianity is powerful. Despite my ardent desire to believe in Islam, I had to admit that history was in favour of Christian claims, and even more reluctantly, that it challenged Islamic teachings.*" Nabeel was not alone on the journey from Islam to Christianity based on the truth claims alone. Abdu Murray followed a similar path of discovery. Abdu said the most significant barrier was not that Christianity was found wanting but feared the effect of converting would have on his family kept him from Christianity. Eventually the pull was too great to resist, and he became a Christian, much to the displeasure of his family.

These are just a few of the books that have fascinated me. They make a robust case for the Christian worldview. I still had many unanswered questions. The central problem I struggled with was why is there evil and suffering in the world? Surely an all-powerful God could do something about this. Epicurus, an ancient Greek philosopher, summed this dilemma up perfectly. *"Is God willing to prevent evil, but not able? Then he is not omnipotent. Is he able, but not willing? Then he is malevolent. Is he both able and willing? Then whence cometh evil? Is he neither able nor willing? Then why call him God?"* Epicurus had a well-reasoned argument. The problem of evil and suffering is undoubtedly one of the most significant barriers to belief. If God exists, should we follow Him or rebel? Why would we follow a God that allowed the slaughter of 190 million people in wars during the 20th century? It seemed that the only way to understand this conundrum is to understand the God of the Bible better (if he exists). The only way I could see how to do this is to read what is purported to be God's revelation to man, that is the Bible.

CHAPTER 3
THE WORLD'S BEST SELLER

*"The book to read is not the one which thinks for
you, but the one which makes you think. No book
in the world equals the Bible for that."*
Harper Lee

*"Men, in a word, must necessarily be controlled, either by a power
within them, or by a power without them; either by the word of God,
or by the strong arm of man; either by the Bible, or by the bayonet."*
Robert Charles Winthrop

*"I read the paper every day and the Bible every day;
that way I know what both sides are up to."*
Zig Ziglar

Why study the Bible?

The Bible is the most universally recognised book in the world. It forms part of Holy Scripture for three of the world's major religions, Judaism, Islam, and Christianity. The Bible is both reverenced and despised. Most people have heard some of the stories in the Bible. Adam and Eve, Noah's ark, David and Goliath, Moses and the ten plagues of Egypt, the birth of Jesus (the Christmas story), and the crucifixion of Jesus (the Easter story). Some of these biblical stories have formed the bases of Hollywood blockbuster movies, although often without authenticity to the original plotline. There is no doubt that the Bible is a unique book. The Bible is a collection of 66 books written by dozens of authors in three languages, Aramaic, Hebrew, and Greek. In total, six hundred thousand words form the Bible. The Bible is divided into two parts, the Old Testament and the New Testament. The Old Testament was written between 1200 and 165 BC and consists of 39 books: the original Hebrew Bible, the sacred scriptures of the Jewish faith. The New Testament was written in the first century AD and consists of 27 books written in Greek, the international language during the New Testament era. The Bible was penned on three continents. The authors were kings, fishermen, tax collectors, farmers, soldiers, princes, doctors, tent makers and diplomats, to name a few. No other book is consistently the world's number one bestseller. It sits in a drawer in most hotel rooms around the world. It has been translated into thousands of languages and dialects.

Are any of these facts an adequate motive to study the Bible? I would say no. The preeminent reason to read the Bible is if the first few words of this ancient book are true. That is, *"In the beginning God created the heaven and the earth,"* Genesis 1:1. If this is true, it raises all kinds of follow-on questions. Who is God? What is his nature? Why did he create humanity? Is He knowable? If these opening lines of this ancient book are right, there is undoubtedly no more critical quest than to find out what this unique book has to say.

As a child, I recall reading the children's Bible. The pictures that portrayed the various stories still vivid in my mind. The Bible always seemed like a great book to read but is any of it true? If so, would it make a difference in my life? It certainly has had a profound effect on the lives of Lee Strobel, Jim Wallace and Nabeel Qureshi as mentioned in previous pages, as well as countless others. Why does what is penned in this ancient book profoundly affects some lives, while others see the Bible as just a collection of stories? I decided to investigate for myself and follow the *"argument wherever it leads."* I did recognise that if I just read the Bible from beginning to end, I would probably come up with the same answers as before. That is, the Bible is a cool book but nothing more. To study the Bible correctly, I would need to enlist the help of teachers of the Bible—such as; Zac Poonen, Chuck Missler and John MacArthur. To get a counter perspective from non-Christians, I would get the views of Bart Ehrman, Christopher Hitchens, Sam Harris and Richard Dawkins to name some of the most outspoken Bible critics. The most significant critic of all was, of course, me. As an engineer most of my working life, I was going to take some convincing that miracles are possible. While I believe that science has not proven how humans ended up existing on earth, I also struggled to believe the Biblical account of how the world was created.

I was, however, prepared to have an open mind. As I read the Bible under the guidance of scholars and teachers', this fascinating book started to unfold and cohere. I began to be aware that I was on an epic literary journey. The Bible begins pre-history with the creation of all matter. There are unbelievably evil acts of murders, rape, incest, betrayal, deception, death of the innocent, the search for good where evil reigns, the rise and fall of mighty empires, predictions of the future and the ultimate act of sacrifice. The Bible talks about other realities outside of our own. I started to see things in the Bible that were hidden before. This ancient book seemed to come alive before me as each page was explained. The significance of bizarre rituals, seemingly meaningless acts and strange story lines were unravelled.

The Bible in brief

The Bible starts prehistory, with God creating the heavens and the earth in six days. The first human pair, Adam and Eve are created at the end of the 6-day creation period. The world was vastly different from that of today. Like contemporary man, Adam and Eve are expected to work. However, the garden they are to gain their living from does not have the same challenges humanity faces today. The land was watered from a constant underwater source, and there are no weeds to contend with. Adam and Eve spend their days tending the garden and in God's company. All this changes when Adam and Eve gave in to Satan's temptation, who appears in a snake's form, tempting the couple to disobey God by eating from a forbidden tree. The tree was the only prohibition that God placed on the couple, not to tempt them but as a way of showing that they loved and trusted God by keeping this one commandment. By this act of defiance, sin enters the world. Men's hearts grow dark as humanity rebels against God. Even here, God's plan for redeeming the people of God is starting to take shape. God addresses the snake and the woman in Genesis 3:15, *"And I will put enmity between you and the woman, and between your seed and her seed; He shall bruise you on the head, And you shall bruise him on the heel."* This passage points to the promise of Jesus' birth, His redeeming work, and His victory over Satan. Because of Adam and Eve's disobedience, the perfect world that Adam and Eve enjoyed was taken away from them. Food production would be harrowing because *"thorns and thistles"* would grow alongside crops. A further foreshadowing of future messianic sacrifice comes when an innocent animal is killed to cover Adam and Eve's nakedness, Genesis 3:21.

Man continues in rebellion to God's will. Cain kills his brother Abel because of jealousy, Genesis 4:8, the first recorded murder. Humanity tries to reach God by building a tower to heaven in Genesis 11:4. Man's wickedness continues until God's patience is finally exhausted. God sends a global flood to the earth to judge man. A righteous family, Noah, his wife, his three sons and their wives, along with all types of animals are saved by building an ark to survive the global flood. The survivors are to repopulate quite a different, post flood earth.

God calls Abraham to follow him with the promise to make him the father of a great nation and that his descendants will be *"like stars in heaven,"* Genesis 22:17. However, Abraham is an old man and still has no children; it seems that God's promise to Abraham will not be fulfilled. Rather than keeping faith in God, Abraham listens to his wife, Sarah, and has a child with Sarah's servant, Hagar, Genesis 16:15. It was a common practice in that part of the world that barren women would have children via their servants. However, God did miraculously give Abraham a son with Sarah named Isaac. To test Abraham's faithfulness, God tells him to offer his son, Isaac, as a sacrifice on Mount Moriah. Just before Abraham offers his son as a human sacrifice, God stops him once Abraham's faith is revealed. A ram, caught in the thicket, is offered as a substitutionary sacrifice in place of his son, Isaac. Again, this is a foreshadowing of the substitutionary sacrifice of Jesus. Mount Moriah is close to the temple mount in Jerusalem. At the peak of Mount Moriah is a place called Golgotha. Again, this foretells future events when another father (God) would offer his son (Jesus) as a sacrifice.

Isaac has a son called Jacob. Jacob goes on to have twelve sons, and their descendants were the twelve tribes of Israel. Joseph is Jacob's favourite child, being the son of his beloved wife, Rachel. This favouritism and Joseph's ability to see the future through dreams causes his siblings to hate him and eventually sell him into slavery because they were envious of him. However, a turn in fortunes leads Joseph to become second in command of Egypt after interpreting

Pharaoh's dreams about an impending famine. God uses Joseph to save his entire family from starvation by moving them to Egypt, where the family grows and prospers.

Hundreds of years later, Jacob's descendants are known as the Israelites and have become slaves in Egypt. Pharaoh was concerned that the Israelites were becoming too numerous and would take over the land one day. To control the Israelite population, Pharaoh orders the killing of all male Israelite babies. To keep her son from being killed, an Israelite woman puts her baby boy in a basket and float's it down the river Nile. She makes sure that Pharaoh's daughter, who bathed in that part of the river saw the child. Pharaoh's daughter pitied the child, raising him as her own. The child is called Moses and was raised as an Egyptian in the house of Pharaoh but never lost his Israelite roots. Eventually, Moses kills an Egyptian who is cruel to an Israelite, forcing him to leave Egypt in fear of his life. After decades away from Egypt, Moses encounters God, who gives Moses his mission to free God's people, the Israelites, from slavery in Egypt. Pharaoh is reluctant to release his slave labour force, the Israelites. Eventually, ten plagues are divinely sent to Egypt, the final and most devastating being the "Angel of Death." The Angel of Death would kill all firstborn, not by nationality but by all that never had the faith to put lamb's blood on the doorposts of their home. The angel would "pass over" anyone with lamb's blood on the doorpost, sparing all the inhabitants inside. Again, this was a foreshadowing of future events. Jesus was also pictured as an innocent lamb, shedding his blood to save others, just like the lamb's blood on the doorposts. Pharaoh' son dies because of this final plague, and so in his grief, Pharaoh agrees to let the Israelites go. Shortly after the Israelites departure, Pharaoh has a change of heart and pursues the Israelites. The Israelites are trapped, the Egyptian army behind and in front, the Red sea. The sea is miraculously divided for the Israelites to cross. When the Egyptian army tries to pursue, the sea returns and drowns the Egyptians. Moses is given the law, known as the Ten

Commandments: the standards and moral code that God's people are supposed to live by.

The first four commandments deal with how man is to interact with God from Exodus 20:2-17, the below is a paraphrase of these laws:-

You shall have no other gods before Me.
You shall not make idols.
You shall not take the name of the Lord your God in vain.
Remember the Sabbath day to keep it holy.

The next six commandments show how men should interact with each other:-

Honour your father and your mother.
You shall not murder.
You shall not commit adultery.
You shall not steal.
You shall not bear false witness against your neighbour.
You shall not covet.

There is a strange episode while the Israelites are wandering in the desert. Poisonous snakes are plaguing the people. Moses is instructed by God to make a brass serpent and put it on a pole on a hill. Anyone that looks at the serpent would not die from the snake bite. Jesus, talking to Nicodemus, later refers to this in John 3:14 saying' *"As Moses lifted up the serpent in the wilderness, even so must the Son of Man be lifted up; so that whoever believes in Him will have eternal life."* Jesus was making a prophecy of His impending crucifixion.

Joshua takes over leadership of the Israelites after Moses death and leads the people into the Promised Land. God raises judges, temporary military leaders like Deborah, Gideon and Samson who protect and fight for God's people. Eventually, the people tire of this leadership, and they call for a King to rule over them. God gives Israel King Saul, King David, and King Solomon. From that point onwards it is all downhill for Israel.

The Kingdom of Israel is divided, and the people start to forget they are God's chosen, turning their back on God. God's prophets like Elijah, Isaiah, Mica and Jeremiah warn that there will be consequences to their wrongdoing if they do not change their ways, but the warnings go unheeded. The divided kingdoms are conquered, and God's people face captivity in foreign lands. People like Daniel and his three friends, Shadrach, Meshach, and Abednego show great courage and stand for God when no one else does, even to the point of facing death in a fiery furnace for their faith. Miraculously they are not harmed and come out of the fire unscathed. Some exiled people returned to the promised land, but God is silent for 400 years, with no prophets, no miracles, and no Angel visitations, marking the period between the New and Old Testament.

The silence is finally broken, first with John the Baptist's birth and then with the nativity of Jesus. Jesus lives a perfect life that teaches truth, love and performs many miracles. He shows the full extent of God's love by taking the place of sinful man and dying on the cross for humanity's sins. He is placed in a tomb, but three days later, Jesus rises from the dead, conquering sin and death.

After witnessing the risen Jesus, His followers are changed from frightened individuals to bold advocates of the risen Jesus. These followers of Christ, now called Christians, travel the world sharing the good news of Jesus love and starting churches. Many of these early Christians die for their faith. The first to be martyred (from the Greek word for witness) is Stephen. The Bible talks about the second coming of Jesus, where He will reign in a new World order. Christians believe they are now part of the story in the continual revelation.

Reading the Bible with fresh eyes, we see that the New Testament is in the Old Testament concealed and the Old Testament is in the

New Testament revealed, as Chuck Missler would say. Chuck is making the point that the whole Bible, even though it is written over hundreds of years and by multiple authors, points to the same integrated message: The Gospel of Jesus Christ.

Evidence in the Bible

The following pages are just a few elements that I have found intriguing when exploring the truth claims made in the Bible. It is by no means meant to be a full-scale analysis of the Bible's authenticity. There are many more complete and more competent works, such as Lee Strobel's book *"The Case for Christ,"* or Jim Wallace's *"Cold Case Christianity,"* to name a few books that I think are very insightful and recommend to you for further study.

Can you prove the Bible?

Is all or part of the Bible true? What about the miracles in this ancient book? These are great questions. It would be illogical to think that we can prove supernatural events like miracles within the realms of a naturalistic World. Miracles are by their very definition outside the normal laws of nature. Obviously, we cannot substantiate the miracles in the Bible like we can prove other naturalistic phenomena, such as gravity. However, there is an abundance of circumstantial evidence which make for a robust case for the Bible's authenticity.

Evaluating the integrity of the Bible

In what manner can we determine what we read in the Bible today is an accurate representation of the original text? How was the Bible conveyed over the centuries? People imagine scribes that copied a page of the Bible would change or add something along the way over the centuries, leading to the current versions of the Bible having little resemblance to the original. The early scribes used to copy manuscripts letter by letter. Every letter was given a numeric value. At the end of each page, the scribe would count the numerical value of the letters. If it did not match the original value, they burned the document and started again to ensure accuracy. How can we prove how accurate these scribes were? The Dead Sea scrolls are a complete copy of the Old Testament, except for the book of Ester. The scrolls were written 100 years before Jesus. The earliest known Bible was written around 900 AD, so there is a 1000 year gap between the two dates. When historians compared the first Bible's accuracy and the Dead Sea scrolls, they found just a 5% difference. These differences were mainly in the spelling of names. The oldest New Testament manuscript found is a fragment of John 18 31:33 called P52. This discovery dates this copy to the 1st century. It is about the size of a credit card written on papyrus; a common writing material used during that period in history. To date, archaeologists have found about 5,800 Greek manuscripts from the New Testament. From these fragments, large parts of the New Testament can be compared with the Bibles we have in circulation today to attest to transmission accuracy over the centuries. It is also possible to piece together the New Testament from the thousands of writings by the early church fathers, referring to the Bible in their literature. These facts indicate that the Bibles that we have today are accurate copies of the originals.

Questions to ask to affirm the reliability of the gospels

Where were the gospels written? Mark's gospel was written in Rome, Luke in Antioch, John in Ephesus, and Matthew in Judea. If all these gospels were penned in so many different locations, how can we be sure that they knew the places they were writing about? If these gospels were eyewitness accounts, we would expect the authors to be familiar with the areas they describe. Despite the gospels being written in varied locations, they should cohere if they are true and accurate accounts. Did the authors know about the geography, agriculture, botany, architecture, traditions, burial practices, economics, law, and culture? The Bible writers were incredibly accurate in these respects, which is what you would expect if these were eyewitness accounts. For example, during the New Testament period, burials were in tombs that were essentially a cave or carved into rock. The body would be covered in spices to disguise the smell of decay. Then a large rock would be placed in front of the tomb. In about a year, the family would recover the bones and put them in a box called an ossuary. This is consistent with the gospel accounts of the tombs that Lazarus and Jesus were laid to rest in. Mary Magdalene and the other women went to Jesus' tomb after the crucifixion to anoint the body of Jesus with spices, again consistent with that era's practices.

You may have heard of other gospels that are not included in the Bible. Why not? The four gospels Matthew, Mark, Luke, and John mention up to 14 villages and towns each, in total 23 places including some exceedingly small places that would not be known about outside the local area (no Google maps back then). If you compare that local knowledge with the gospel of Philip, it only mentions Jerusalem and Nazareth. The gospel of Peter mentions only Jerusalem, yet other later gospels do not mention any place names. The four New Testament gospels mention the place names in a very matter of fact way and not in a contrived fashion to make the accounts sound authentic.

Do the Gospel writers use the right names?

It is a well-known fact that different countries and regions have different popularities in names. By way of an example, it is rare for an Englishmen to be called Dimitris; likewise, it is unusual for a Cypriot to be called Charles. This is true for first-century Palestine. Specific names are common in eastern cultures because of the tradition of honouring family members by calling their offspring after them. In Luke 1:60, Elizabeth, the mother of John the Baptist was dedicating her son in the temple. The priest asked what the child should be called, she said his name was to be John. Her relatives protested, *"There is no one among your relatives who is called by that name,"* Luke 1:60. This was an expected response in a culture where names and honour are important.

The "Tal Ilan: The Lexicon of Jewish names in later antiquity" is a study of the common names in and around first-century Jewish Palestine. In 2003, a comparison of names in the Lexicon was made with names in the New Testament with remarkable results. It was found that there is an accuracy within 1% of name usage (41% vs 40% in the New Testament). The most common names for men were Simon, Joseph, Lazarus, Judas, John, Jesus, and Ananias. When these common names are used in the Bible, and when it is not obvious which one the writer is referring to, a qualifier is used. For example, John is one of the common names, and so a qualifier is used. There is John the Baptist, or John, the brother of James. When the daughter of Herodias pleases Herod, she says, *"Give me the head of John the Baptist here on a platter,"* Matthew 14:8. She does not want any John's head, and to save confusion, she tells Herod exactly which John's head she wants. Again, when Simon is used, a qualifier follows the name. There is Simon the zealot and Simon Peter, the disciple of Jesus. This pattern goes on and on for other popular names in first-century Palestine. By way of a modern-day example, my wife's grandfather was called George. Following eastern tradition, seven of grandfather's eight children named their offspring either George or Georgia. To distinguish between them, they were given nicknames so you could individually address them. There is Magic George (because he does magic), Little George (because he is the youngest), Fuego George (because he used to drive a Renault Fuego), the list goes on. And then, of course, I joined the family to add to the confusion. I was dubbed Lulu's George (after my wife). It is amusing to see all the heads turn when at family gatherings someone calls out "George" without the qualifier. When an uncommon name is used in first-century Palestine, there is no qualifier to distinguish that person. For example, Philip, one of the disciples, has no qualifier when his name is quoted in the New Testament. Why? He is number 61 in the list of popular names and unlikely to be confused with others. The sequence is repeated with Bartholomew, Thaddeus and Thomas, all unpopular names and so no qualifiers. Interestingly, when Jewish male names in Egypt a few miles away are considered, the popular names there are Eleazar, Joseph, Josephus, and Samul. These do not feature prominently in the New Testament, suggesting that the gospel writers wrote about real people in a small part of the Middle East, adding to the gospel accounts' authenticity.

Does history agree with the Bible?

The Bible's authenticity is questioned regularly because of doubts that some of the Bible's characters and places mentioned did not actually exist. The reason for the scepticism is because there is often no extra-biblical evidence. The Hittites were mentioned several times in books of the Bible, for example, in the book of Judges, Exodus and Joshua; however, the Hittite empire was not mentioned in any other historical text, and no tangible evidence existed. Many people cited this as evidence that the Bible was inaccurate. However, in 1906-1908, Hugo Winckler, a German archaeologist, discovered that the Hittites did exist when he excavated the Hittite capital at Hattusa in the modern-day town of Bogazkale in Turkey.

Belshazzar appears in the book of Daniel as the King of Babylon. However, there was no extra-biblical literary or physical evidence of his existence. Is this story just a legend, or does the Bible preserve accurate history? Some sceptics denied that there ever was a King of Babylon named Belshazzar, claiming that his name and story was invented by someone unfamiliar with real Babylonian history. It looked like all the evidence was stacked against the accuracy of the Bible. Then a series of archaeological discoveries showed that Belshazzar did exist after all, and the details given about him in the Bible are profoundly accurate.

There has been considerable doubt about the existence of King

Solomon. The Bible talks about significant building work that Solomon undertook, so it would seem reasonable that evidence of this work should exist. Archaeological clues have been found, dating back to the 10th century BC (the Solomon era) of major building work at Hazor, Megiddo and Gezer. These archaeological finds are by no means conclusive evidence but seem consistent with Solomon's building projects as recorded in the Bible.

These are just a few examples where the Bible and history concur. The Bible has proved so reliable historically that it is often used as a point of reference by historians and archaeologists when discoveries have been made around the areas the Bible portrays.

The first eyewitnesses to the resurrection are women

As 21st-century westerners living in a society of equal gender rights, we may miss completely the fact that the first to witness the risen Jesus were women. This may seem insignificant, but it took two women's testimony to equate to a man's in Jewish circles. If the resurrection accounts were fabricated, the last people you would use as the first witnesses would have been women, especially a woman like Mary Magdalene with her chequered career. When Paul recounts the eyewitnesses of the resurrection in 1 Corinthians 15:5, he says, *"He (Jesus) appeared to Cephas, then to the twelve. After that He appeared to more than five hundred brethren at one time, most of whom remain until now, but some have fallen asleep; then He appeared to James, then to all the apostles; and last of all, as to one untimely born, He appeared to me also."* It is as if Paul, with his pharisaic upbringing, is without consciously thinking about it naming all the "credible" eyewitnesses from a legal standpoint. That did not include women.

Evidence of embarrassment

The Gospels have what is called evidence of embarrassment, which refers to evidence showing witnesses in a poor light which would only be included if true, due to the embarrassing details. For example, the fact that women were the first witnesses. That the disciples were fearful and so ran away rather than face the possibility of retribution themselves all serve as embarrassing evidence for the resurrection account. People will not own up to something that puts them in poor standing unless of course, it happens to be true.

Sweating blood

In Luke 22:44, there is a curious sentence that occurs while Jesus is praying before his crucifixion, *"And being in agony, He was praying very fervently; and His sweat became like drops of blood, falling down upon the ground."* Who has ever seen sweat like blood? Surely if someone were fabricating this account, you would not add something that no one has ever seen? Unless of course the Bible writers wrote what they saw and saw what they wrote. It is only recently that medicine has discovered a condition called hematidrosis. The condition occurs when the capillary blood vessels feeding the sweat glands rupture, causing them to exude blood and the sufferer "sweats blood." The occurrences are rare and only manifest themselves under extreme physical or emotional stress, for example an impending crucifixion.

Transformation of the early disciples

On the night of the crucifixion, the disciples (except John) did not want to be associated with Jesus for fear of reprisals. Most notably was Peter. He declared to Jesus that *"Even if they all fall away because of You, I will never fall away!"* Matthew 26:33. The other disciples disappeared into the shadows of Jerusalem and out of the next few pages of the New Testament. Peter actively denied knowing Jesus on three occasions despite his earlier pledge of allegiance, Matthew 26:69-74. Within a few weeks, Peter boldly professes the crucified Jesus to a large crowd in the book of Acts. What was it that changed Peter and his fellow disciples from frightened individuals? Helpfully Peter explains it was witnessing the risen Jesus. Acts 2:24 *"But God raised Him up again, putting an end to the agony of death since it was impossible for Him to be held in its power."*

We have probably all met people whose lives have been transformed by some life-changing event. It could be surviving a life-threatening disease or a near-fatal car accident. It tends to make people appreciate life and change their lives, for example, raising money for charity or living life more fully. The most remarkable account I have heard is that of a young army officer involved in a serious road traffic accident. He had an out of body experience, looking at the paramedics trying to revive his mangled body. He recalls a remarkable conversation he had with what the young army officer assumed was an angelic being who told him he would live; however, his life would never be the same. The paramedics declared their efforts futile and stopped trying to revive him. Several days later, the young army officer startled the morgue workers by twitching his toe. Clearly, he was in the morgue because the medical professionals had pronounced him dead at the scene of the accident. After several operations and a year's recuperation, the young army officer made a miraculous recovery and, as a result, left his promising career in the military to be a minister of the church. This account is fantastic and outside what we usually experience. Whether you believe this story or not, clearly, it was an event that changed the young army officer's life because he did believe his experience was real. In the same way, what the disciples witnessed changed their lives. John Stott said, *"If anything is clear from the Gospels and the Acts it is that the apostles were sincere. They may have been deceived, if you like, but they were not deceivers. Hypocrites and martyrs are not made of the same stuff."*

The missing motive

It is a popular theory that the Bible was written to control people during the dark days of the ancient world and that Jesus had no intention of starting a religion. However, his followers did. Is there evidence of this? As Jim Wallace says, all crime can be attributed to three motives, relationships, greed, or power. The early Christians had none of those motives. They were subsequently impoverished for their beliefs, handing over money to a common purse for the collective good. The early Christians were vilified wherever they went because they had turned their back on Judaism to be counted followers of Jesus. Reading the experiences of Muslims converting to Christianity, like Nabeel Qureshi, you get a sense of what a seismic event it would have been for easterners. This traumatic experience would have been replicated for first-century Jews to convert to Christianity. It would mean that they could no longer blend in with the culture around them. It would be difficult for them to trade with the Jews or find partners for themselves and their children. They would, in no uncertain terms, be ostracised. They would surely not do this for a lie.

Willingness to die

Something happened to transform the disciples' lives from frightened men to being willing to die for their beliefs. Peter was crucified upside down, Thomas speared to death, Stephen, the first martyr, was stoned to death. Paul was a persecutor of the church, a zealous Pharisee, he changed to being the greatest advocate of Christianity, writing about a third of the New Testament. Paul was later beheaded for his beliefs. Would they sacrifice so much for a lie? These early Christians are not alone in dying for their faith. The 19 Muslims that carried out the 9/11 attacks in the US also died for what they believed. The difference is what these Muslims believed and thus motivated them is not something that they directly witnessed, unlike these early Christians. N. T. Wright notes in his classic book, *The Resurrection of the Son of God*, that, "*the disciples had no theological motivation behind claiming that Jesus had risen from the dead as they were anticipating a military hero and a final resurrection at the end of time.*" *What motivating factors existed for these disciples to invent such a story? None! The only reason the disciples taught the resurrection of Jesus was because Jesus's resurrection had occurred."*

Final analysis

It is a common belief that the Bible was written centuries after the events it portrays in its pages. The argument proposed is that there is the possibility that the Bible has errors in copying—the potential for legends to appear and even wilfully corrupted to suit the rich and powerful. A common theme is that the Catholic Church has corrupted the Bible to control people. If an investigative approach is adopted to discover the Bible's authenticity, this is found not to be the case. The Bible has proved to be able to stand up to the most rigorous of scrutiny. On close inspection, the New Testament was written within living memory of the events it depicts, and some scholars believe within a few years. This would eliminate the chance of legend being formed, which is possible if there is a long time between the historical events and the eventual documenting. Does this reliability of transmission mean that the content is authentic? The two do not necessarily follow.

There are multitudes of surviving mythological writings from cultures all over the ancient world, but that does not make the contents of these books true. Does this reasoning apply to the Bible? After all, the Bible also has some fantastic events that are outside the human experience of today. Think the virgin birth, parting of the Red sea and the raising of the dead. Even if the Bible can be proven trustworthy in its origin, can we expect people to believe all it says? Just as we would not expect people to believe in a winged horse called Pegasus from Greek mythology, would we expect people to believe the Bible's miracles? It is reasonable then that people reading the Bible would have reservations about its pages' supernatural events. Should we only believe in the natural world and scientifically provable things? The philosopher David Hume wrote, *"When we run over libraries, persuaded of these principles, what havoc must we make? If we take in our hand any volume—of divinity or school metaphysics, for instance—let us ask, does it contain any abstract reasoning concerning quantity or number? No. Does it contain any experimental reasoning concerning matter of fact and existence? No. Commit it then to the flames, for it can contain nothing but sophistry and illusion."* The problem with this statement is it does not fit into either category, so it is self-defeating. Should this statement also be "committed to the flames?" Sceptics need to be open minded to the possibility of the supernatural, even if they remain sceptical. To be closed to this possibility is to claim absolute knowledge of the universe—an astounding "godlike" claim, a claim we cannot make without knowing all that is knowable.

Albert Einstein, the German born physicist maintained that we humans still only know a tiny fraction of what is knowable. Are we then to discount anything in life that has a supernatural explanation? In the four dimensions we live in, can we humans be sure that it is not possible for intervention into our universe from the other six dimensions that "string theory" postulates? The main stumbling block that people will site are the miracles in the Bible. Of course, this is an understandable reaction as we do not see virgins conceive. That is why Joseph reacted the way he did initially. He knew where babies come from, so he wanted to send Mary away as he believed a naturalistic answer to Mary's pregnancy. We do not see dead men rise and live again. It is for this very reason why Thomas, the disciple of Jesus, said he would not believe that Jesus had risen from the dead *"Unless I see in His hands the imprint of the nails, and put my finger into the place of the nails, and put my hand into His side, I will not believe."* John 20:24. These are genuine reactions to supernatural events that we would expect. Just as if we were told of virgins conceiving or the dead walking today, we would not believe. Of course, the greatest miracle of all is how we all came into existence.

As briefly discussed in earlier chapters, the finely tuned universe we occupy, why there is something rather than nothing can all be classed as supernatural and outside of what we usually experience. Are these events miracles? Can we humans claim to know everything there is to know? Science's best guess on how the universe came to be is equally fantastic. However, because it is labelled "science," the explanations are accepted without considering how implausible these statements are. Stephen Hawking says, *"Because there is a law such as gravity, the universe can and will create itself from nothing."* A self-assembling universe does seem to be hard to believe as nothing does, well, nothing. I purchased some furniture from a well-known Swedish furniture shop. The furniture came flat packed with a big sign on the side of the box saying "self-assembly." I remember watching the box for hours. Nothing happened, so I had to assemble it myself. While I am being flippant, this rather poor attempt at humour highlights the fact that self-assembling universes are beyond the realms of any science that we currently know.

I remember my religious education teacher trying to explain the virgin birth as Mary being a temple helper. My teacher said that it was legitimate for the priest to have relationships with her. This was based on absolutely no fact. My teacher tried to explain away the angels the shepherds saw at Jesus nativity as butterflies. It would be miraculous for men that lived close to nature all their lives to be fooled into thinking butterflies were angelic beings. These are admittedly extreme examples but highlight a world where anything is to be believed rather than the possibility of a God. A God who has the power to intervene in the normal laws of nature and perform acts contrary to the ordinary workings of the universe.

In the final analysis, the Bible makes some incredible claims outside our usual understanding, as does science. The current explanations for how life and the universe came into existence seem fantastic. Science postulates that everything came from nothing, so it is a question of which virgin birth you believe. Either the birth of a universe from nothing or the Son of God's birth from a virgin. We all have the same evidence; it is how we explain our existence from that evidence. A poor example of this is the letters GODISNOWHERE.

Depending on where you put the spaces makes all the difference. You can read this as GOD IS NO WHERE or GOD IS NOW HERE. Same letters, but quite a different conclusion. From reading the Bible, do you conclude that **GOD IS NO WHERE, or GOD IS NOW HERE?**

The Bible message

The Bible message is unique amongst the world's religions. While it is always a danger to summarise religions, they tend to have one thing in common. Most religious systems involve humanity trying to be good enough to be acceptable to God. A person's good deeds need to outweigh their bad to make themselves righteous. In the Bible, God is reaching out to humankind while acknowledging that man can never be good enough in his own merit in our fallen state. God comes to earth as a human. Born of a virgin, Jesus experiences human frailties but lives a perfect, sinless life. As a perfect example, Jesus can justify man by taking on the sins of the world, dying on the cross so that humanity can be in perpetual union with the triune God.

The road to Damascus

While my story so far has been written in a few short pages, it has taken a lifetime of careful thought to draw the inferences I have. The more I contemplate life and how humanity ended up on this ball we call earth hurtling through space, the more incredible I find our very existence. My discovery journey started as a child when I was forced to go to church, not understanding a word of the Greek Orthodox service and thinking that the priest's rituals were pointless. As I grew and started looking into science, thinking that it had the answers I was looking for, I was so surprised that behind the big words and even thicker books that scientists produced, they are no closer to answering the fundamental question of how we came to be. Science is even less forthcoming when it came to answering the "why" questions.

Why are we here? John Lennox, a Christian scientist, famously said that scientists could tell you what a cake is made of and how the ingredients changed during the cooking process. Scientists can work out the cake's calorific and nutritional value, however, no scientist can explain why the cake is there in the first place. Only the cake's baker can do that. It could be a grandmother baking the cake to surprise her grandchild for no other reason than the love she has for her granddaughter. On the other hand, and to my surprise, the Bible provided meaning to life. Rather than being a relic of history, it showed relevance to our lives today. It signposted the way to live life, purpose for living as well as pointing to our origins and our ultimate destination.

There you have it. In case you have not spotted the transition as the pages of this book have unfolded, I now believe in the gospel message. Like Saint Paul on the road to Damascus, I began the journey thinking Christianity could not be true and then gradually, the evidence seemed overwhelming. It was not a dramatic conversion like Saint Paul's Road to Damascus encounter with Jesus. None the less it was a realisation and then acceptance of the gospel message.

As a nominal Christian from birth, I remember meeting born again Christians. They made me feel uncomfortable as it seemed that every aspect of their lives had a Christian overtone to it. Why were they not like other nominal Christians I knew and kept God in a box until Sunday and let Him out for a couple of hours? Or if they needed something, say a prayer or two to ask for what they need? I think the issue is most people do not want a God; they want a genie, a wishful filler; they do not want someone to be ultimately accountable to during the final reckoning. There is a problem with this approach. If there is a God, and I think the previous pages should at least open the possibility that there may be, then what does He want with us? His role cannot be to keep us topped up with prayer requests. People will often bargain with God. Offering God something in return for fulfilling a prayer request. This is a strange concept when you think of it logically. What could we possibly offer the God of creation that He needs? This reminds me of a scene in Star Trek V: The Final Frontier. The crew of the Enterprise have found "god". This "god" wants to make use of the starship. When James T Kirk waves a hand in the air to get "gods" attention to address him. Kirks says, *"Excuse me... excuse me, I would just like to ask a question. What does god need with a starship?"* I am not sure if theology is part of the Star Fleet Academy curriculum, but Kirk obviously understands that a true God has no need of anything made.

The more I think about my life and my purpose, the more I understand my role and why I am here. I realise I am not here to live 60, 70, 80, 90 years, raise some kids, retire to the coast, and become the ultimate statistic, that is, 10 out of 10 die. I am convinced that life is more than this, and I hope you will continue turning the pages of this book and *"follow the argument wherever it leads,"* as Socrates would say, rather than having a preconceived mindset.

I suspect that some of you will not carry-on reading. I hope that is not the case. Some may say he is a Christian now; the book has no more relevance for me. It is full of out of date hocus pocus anti-scientific nonsense. I hope that is not you, and you continue this journey to discover the truth. If you persevere with this book, you will see the significance of the Christian life and how it answers the most fundamental questions we all ask. Where did I come from (origin)? Why am I here (meaning)? How do I live my life (morality)? Where do I go when this mortal life is over (destiny)?

CHAPTER 4
WORLDVIEWS

"Nothing is more dangerous than a dogmatic worldview."
Stephen Jay Gould

"Your worldview has to have the same shape that reality does."
J. Budziszewski

"Hope is what you get when you suddenly realize that a different worldview is possible, a worldview in which the rich, the powerful, and the unscrupulous do not after all have the last word. The same worldview shift that is demanded by the resurrection of Jesus is the shift that will enable us to transform the world."
N. T. Wright

Origin, Meaning, Morality and Destiny

Everyone has a worldview. That is a personal philosophy of life and conception of the world. A person's worldview will determine how they interact with others, colour decisions and opinions they form and draw conclusions from life.

A person's worldview needs to answer these four fundamental questions; where we come from (origin), why are we here (meaning), how do we live our lives (morality), and where do we go (destiny). A person's worldview needs to be tested to see how it answers these four crucial questions. Are the answers internally consistent? Do they correspond to reality and most importantly, are they liveable? Atheism's answer to these four questions are; we came from nothing, we have no purpose, there is no morality, and we go nowhere. I believe that this worldview is contributing to the chaos in our world today. The Oxford dictionary word of the year for 2016 was "post-truth" which reflects a world where you can say anything if it makes you "feel" good. It does not need to reflect the reality of truth. In fact, in recent years, the truth has been the casualty of modern society. The millennials find it particularly difficult not to be plagued by popularism. They are pressured to "like" what the world likes rather than what God likes. Social media bombards them with how they should look, behave and what to tolerate.

The following pages are thoughts that I have put together on these crucial subjects from a Christian worldview. I think you will find that no other worldview has such a complete answer to these four questions. Unlike our atheist friends, the Christian worldview is that we were created for a purpose; we are not an accident. We were created on purpose and for a purpose. We are to live our lives according to the laws prescribed by God, not to hinder our freedom but to enshrine our rights and protect them through His laws. The purpose of our lives is not to live for ourselves, but God. Our ultimate objective is to restore fellowship with God and to be with Him in heaven for eternity.

"If you look at the world, you'll be distressed. If you look within, you'll be depressed. But if you look at Christ, you'll be at rest." Corrie ten Boom

Origin

Genesis 1:1, *"In the beginning God created the heavens and the earth."*

> *"God made all of His creation to give. He made the sun, the moon, the stars, the clouds, the earth, the plants to give. He also designed His supreme creation, man, to give. But fallen man is the most reluctant giver in all of God's creation."* John MacArthur

Understanding origins is critical to understanding human behaviour. If we humans do not know where we come from, we cannot comprehend what we are here for (meaning), how we interact with each other (morality) or where we go ultimately (destiny). There are just two options on origins, either there is a God who created everything, or there is not. If God exists, he created man, if not, man created God! If there is no God, where do we come from? The famous scientist Stephen Hawking of Cambridge University said on the subject, *"The universe can and will create itself from nothing. Spontaneous creation is the reason there is something rather than nothing, why the universe exists, why we exist."* The atheist Philosopher Quentin Smith said, *"The fact of the matter is that the most reasonable belief is that we came from nothing, by nothing and for nothing . . . We should . . . acknowledge our foundation in nothingness and feel awe at the marvellous fact that we have a chance to participate briefly in this incredible sunburst that interrupts without reason the reign of non-being.*" In short, the atheist's answer is we came from "nothing." What exactly is nothing? The ancient Greek philosopher Aristotle said that *"Nothing is what rocks dream of."* There have been many debates on what "nothing" is exactly by many prominent thinkers. At first glance this seems an easy concept to grasp. That is, empty space can be deemed as "nothing." Neil deGrasse Tyson, director of the Hayden Planetarium, said, *"If laws of physics still apply, the laws of physics are not nothing."* Clearly even in space, the laws of physics still apply.

Atheism believes that humans are merely physical; they have no soul and no spirit. While I completely understand that the concept of a creator God is a challenging notion for humans to grasp, the alternative, we come from nothing, seems more puzzling to understand conceptually. I have to say that I do not have enough faith to be persuaded that nothing has created everything. I believe nothing is precisely that, nothing. Nothing has never done anything in the past and never will in the future. Where does that lead us? If we disagree with prominent thinkers of the 21st century, what is the alternative? The logical conclusion is God created everything; if so, what does he want with us, how do we get to know Him and His purpose for us? He gave us the 66 books of the Bible that tell us how the world was created, why the world was created, why the world has gone so wrong, what was done to put things right, and how the current world order will end. Does that mean I never have doubts? Never have questions? No, every day of the week I have my doubts, but the more I seek answers in the Bible and prayer, the more I understand where I came from and my purpose for existing. I am in particularly good company when it comes to doubts. John the Baptist leapt inside his mother's womb when he heard the news of Jesus' miraculous conception when Mary addressed Elizabeth, Luke 1:41. John later saw the spirit of God descending on Jesus at His baptism. With all of this first-hand experience John, while in prison, still had doubts. He struggled to understand why he was left to languish in a damp dungeon if Jesus was the promised messiah and so sent his disciples to ask, *"Are You the Coming One, or are we to look for someone else?"* Matthew 11:3.

Why did God create the world? It was not for love, as He already had love through the Trinity, the Father, Son and Holy Spirit. Even though God did not need to create us, He delighted to do so. We often do many things that are not necessary, like having children. We may be pleased with our marriage, but we still desire to procreate and have the joy of children. It is not necessary, but it is an experience filled with joy.

Here are some thoughts as to why God created us.

- To be stewards over creation
- To be His chosen people and testimony to the nations
- That we might bring Him glory and praise
- That He might delight in us and we in Him
- To know Him and be known by Him

"I believe in the Big Bang. I just know who "banged" it!" Frank Turek

Meaning

Mark 12 29-31," *Love the Lord your God with all your heart and with all your soul and with all your mind and with all your strength.' The second is this: 'Love your neighbour as yourself.' There is no commandment greater than these."*

"The greatest tragedy is not death, but life without purpose." Rick Warren

In 2002, a TV advert showed a woman in a hospital about to give birth to a baby boy. She gives a final scream, and the baby shoots out of the hospital window. Viewers then see the baby boy ageing rapidly as he is propelled through the air screaming, suggesting a traumatic experience, before crashing into a grave. The advert ends with the tolling of a church bell and a caption saying: *"Life is short. Play more XBOX."* While this advert was in poor taste (it had several complaints and so no longer screened) and trivialised life's purpose (playing games), Microsoft suggested this was a positive message. Can this really be the purpose of life? While this is clearly an over trivialisation of life, it highlights that people are looking for purpose and that a game can be thought of as that purpose is quite sad.

How are we supposed to live? What is the meaning or purpose of life? Most people live their lives for themselves, accumulating as much wealth, partners, places of honour in society as they can. People are always looking for the next new high; to go on more exotic holidays, a better smartphone, a more attractive lover etc. The problem is, after every new high, you end up on a new low. All these temporal things leave a person unfulfilled. For example, you visit a beautiful country in Europe, next year returning to the same place will not do, you need to visit a more exotic country. You need a new high; then you get a new low. This cycle goes on as these worldly experiences can never fill the space where God is supposed to occupy. Ravi Zacharias, an apologist, puts this beautifully, *"The older you get the more it takes to fill your heart with wonder, and only God is big enough to fill that heart of ours."* Life is not about us! It is about living for God. To glorify God in everything we say and do.

Statistics show that generally, those who live for God are happier, healthier and more content with their lives, than those who live for material wealth and the pleasures of this world. It is not that the Christian tries to escape living on earth by thinking of heaven, but this life makes more sense by realising that life is a trial for the next stage of our existence. It is like an exam that we all sit with a finite time to complete the test. Once you realise that is the purpose of life it gives you the right perspective on material things.

People say they will die for their loved ones, but would they live for them? Be there for them, give up drinking, give up smoking and spend time in God's word with them? When people look at you, do they think that God is optional or essential? A person is either growing or dying! Physiologically we are all dying, but spiritually we should be growing. How can you tell your priorities in life? Just look at your bank account and your diary! Do you spend time with God in prayer? Do you give your money to help the needy or spend it on yourself?

Morality

Matthew 7:12 "In everything, therefore, treat people the same way you want them to treat you, for this is the Law and the Prophets."

> *"The moral absolutes rest upon God's character. The moral commands He has given to men are an expression of His character. Men as created in His image are to live by choice on the basis of what God is. The standards of morality are determined by what conforms to His character, while those things which do not conform are immoral." Francis Schaeffer*

Having one of my in-depth philosophical discussions with a friend of mine, we somehow got onto the subject of morality. The conversation quickly moved on to the Nuremberg trials that took place at the end of the second World War. A familiar cry of the defendants was, "I was just following orders." My question to my friend was, is this sufficient justification for their actions? Based on the morality of the Nazi party, they were doing nothing wrong in acting out the genocide of the Jewish race. Where did the Allies get their morality from, and were they right to judge the Nazis based on the Allies standard of right and wrong? My friend's response was because the Allies won the war, they had the right to judge the Nazis.

I was not comfortable with this notion. What if the Nazis had won the war? Did that make their morality correct, and so by extension, the genocide of the Jews would have been morally right? How do we define what is evil and what is good? How do we decide what moral law is? For the new atheist Richard Dawkins this is easy, he says, *"The universe we observe has precisely the properties we should expect if there is, at bottom, no design, no purpose, no evil, no good, nothing but blind, pitiless indifference."* Is there really no evil?

If you look around what one person sees as immoral, another person sees as OK. I remember being in a Muslim country, it was just after Friday prayers, so the worshipers were exiting the mosques. A young western lady was walking in their midst, scantily dressed. She was getting all kinds of looks of disapproval from the worshipers. If this lady were to be placed anywhere else in the west, she would have hardly been noticed. Should morality be based on where she is in the world? Yet another example was told to me by a stewardess. She said that while on duty on a flight from Riyadh, Saudi Arabia, a young man and two women boarded the flight as first-class passengers wearing traditional modest Arab dress. Just after take-off, the man and two women went to the toilets and got changed into clearly expensive western clothes. They started drinking alcohol throughout the flight. This story's point is not to offend our Muslim friends but to highlight that where the trio was in the world affected their behaviour. A final example was told to me by a Yemenis lady. She told me the story of a westerner drinking a can of coke during the month of Ramadan, teasing the locals as they were not allowed to drink or eat during the period of fasting. The locals were so enraged at the man's taunting that they beat him senseless. Should the westerner respect the locals' religious beliefs? Did the Yemenis have the right to retaliate for the provocation? Was the retaliation disproportionate to the offence?

I believe I cannot even trust my own level of morality. An example of this was as a child we heard of a relative of ours going through a divorce. We were all shocked at the prospect. My mother tried desperately to persuade the relative to change her mind. Years later, divorce does not shock or surprise me. I could give numerous other examples of my changing morality, sometimes going full circle as the years go by. This proves that my own standards of morality cannot be trusted let alone that of the world around me.

How do you define what is evil? By defining what is good. What is good? If there is no absolute moral law and no moral lawgiver, then one person's good is another man's evil. For example, some people's morals dictate that you love your neighbour; others believe it is every man for himself, in other cultures, cannibals eat their neighbours! Which one do you prefer? If moral law is a personal preference, everyone has a different standard which will inevitably cause divisions. The examples in the last paragraph highlight this in real-life situations. If evil is purely what a person believes to be evil, then all we need do is to change our minds on evil. Evil is not the presence of something. Evil is the absence of righteousness.

Friedrich Nietzsche, the 19th Century German Philosopher and atheist, coined the phrase "God is dead." Nietzsche said that because God had "died" in the 19th Century, the 20th Century would be the bloodiest, most catastrophically destructive Century in history. He was right. What drove Nietzsche to say this? While Nietzsche did not believe in God, he did recognise that the lack of consistent moral standards would lead to widespread destruction, which of course, was the case as the 20th Century unfolded. Over 190 million were killed in two world wars and other bloody atrocities such as Stalin's purge in the Soviet Union.

People will often say that God wants to limit individual's freedom, giving us all kinds of laws to restrict us. True freedom is only possible under rules and regulations. If you do not break these rules, you are free to do anything within those limits. These rules are not there to limit our freedom but to protect it. For example, if you abide by the Highway Code, you can go anywhere in the country in safety. However, if someone says I want to be free to do anything I want and drives down the wrong way of a motorway, his supposed freedom could result in taking a life. If you go beyond the freedom that God has given us (sin), you need to pay for your actions either in this life or the next.

I think it is clear. The more humans try to invent their morality, the more conflict there is between us. You only have to look at human history to see this played out with bloody consequences. There are almost as many standards of morality in this world as there are people. The only way we as humans can genuinely get along with each other is to have a common law outside of ourselves. That is God's law as defined in the Bible.

> *"Reading the Bible will keep you from sin or sin*
> *will keep you from the Bible." D L Moody*

Destiny

Philippians 3:20 *"For our citizenship is in heaven, from which we also eagerly wait for a Saviour, the Lord Jesus Christ."*

> *"The way to Heaven is ascending; we must be content*
> *to travel uphill, though it be hard and tiresome, and*
> *contrary to the natural bias of our flesh." Jonathan*
> *Edwards*

As the last few pages of this book have unfolded, we can see where we have come from (origin), why we are here (meaning) and how to interact with each other (morality) but ultimately what is this life all about? I believe life is not just the 80 or 90 years we live on this earth; these mortal years are a test to see where we should ultimately go in our final form of the resurrected body. It is the destiny of our soul that is all-important. That is, either to spend an eternity in the presence of God or not.

I have often heard people say that they would not like to go to heaven as it looks "boring" with everyone dressed in white playing the harp. Boring is the one thing I do not believe heaven will be. Imagine being able to know all the secrets of the universe. John 21:25 says, *"But there are also many other things which Jesus did, which, if they were written in detail, I expect that even the world itself would not contain the books that would be written."* Imagine being able to learn first-hand from the maker.

We need to be heaven centred, not earth centred. We should be like Abraham, *"vagabonds on the earth"* as the earth is not our home. It is like going on holiday and spending time and money decorating your hotel room and neglecting your real home! In this analogy, the hotel is the earth, and our real home is heaven! However, we should make sure that we are not "so heavenly minded that we are no earthly good." If someone is dying of thirst, he does not need a sermon; he needs a glass of water. We should spend our time on earth wisely, *"storing up treasures in heaven."* What are these treasures? I believe these are the good deeds that we do, not that salvation is of works, but you cannot be a Christian and live as the world does. You will want to share the good news, to evangelise to the world. We should be bursting at the seams to proclaim the message of salvation to a world in need. I believe that evangelism is the greatest treasure you can store in heaven. I do not believe that evangelism is dependent on any single human being. Not witnessing to someone does not frustrate God's plan for that person's salvation. After all, the scriptures say that all those saved have their name written in the book of life before the world's foundation. I do believe, however, that evangelism is a privilege that God gives all His children. In heaven, we will delight in people we have witnessed to. So, make sure that your life in heaven is full of rejoicing for those you saved. After all, eternity is a long time to be reflecting on what might have been. Earth is touched by heaven and hell. For Christians, the earth is the closest they will come to hell, and for an atheist, it is the closest they will come to heaven.

Stephen Hawking, the famous scientist, once said, *"Heaven is a fairy story for those afraid of the dark.*" John Lennox, a Christian scientist, replied, *"Atheism is a fairy story for those afraid of the light."* While in heaven, we will no longer weep because there will be nothing to make us sad. There will be no more murder because there will be no one to hate. There will be no more arguments because there will be nothing to argue about. In short, heaven is a place of perfect joy. No longer will we envy, lust, or covet. It is a place of perfect bliss and constant communion with God.

There are all kinds of conjecture on what hell is like, causing theologians to debate endlessly. Is it a fiery furnace? A place of darkness? Is it separation from God or a place of eternal torment? To which I say I do not know the answer. All I do know is I do not want to go there to find out.

"Aim at heaven and you will get earth thrown in. Aim at earth and you get neither." C. S. Lewis

CHAPTER 5
LIVING YOUR LIFE

*"The Christian shoemaker does his duty not by putting
little crosses on the shoes, but by making good shoes,
because God is interested in good craftsmanship."*
Martin Luther

"Worry is the darkroom in which negatives can develop."
Wanda E. Brunstetter

*"When we teach our children to be good, to be gentle, to be
forgiving (all these are attributes of God), to be generous, to love
their fellow men, to regard this present age as nothing, we instil
virtue in their souls, and reveal the image of God within them."*
John Chrysostom

Ten parts to Christian living

Acts 11:26, "And the disciples were first called Christians in Antioch"

> *"The Christian life is not a constant high. I have my*
> *moments of deep discouragement. I have to go to God*
> *in prayer with tears in my eyes, and say, 'O God,*
> *forgive me,' or 'Help me."* Billy Graham

As mentioned before in this book, it is a common belief that all roads lead to God and that all religions are fundamentally the same but superficially different. The inference being it does not matter what deity you believe. Is this true? Well, I am quite sure no one believes in the ancient Egyptian sun god Ra anymore. What happened to all those ancients that believed in and worshipped Ra? Today Hindus worship a whole multitude of gods and goddesses. Buddhist do not believe in God. So, are all religions fundamentally the same but superficially different? It is the other way around. They are fundamentally different and superficially similar. You can replace the Buda from Buddhism, Mohammed from Islam. It would not make a material difference to that faith. However, you cannot replace Jesus from Christianity. Jesus and Christianity are unique. No other religion claims to have the son of God, making Jesus equal to God as the central character of that belief system. No other faith has God suffering and dying at the hands of His creation to redeem them for no other reason than love for His creation. You can go to the grave of the Buda or Mohammed, but you cannot go to the tomb of Jesus. People that die and come back to life have something worth saying, *"He who has ears to hear, let him hear."* Mark 4:9. Jesus himself claimed exclusivity in John 14:6; He said, *"I am the way, the truth and the life. No one comes to the Father except through Me."* A clear rebuttal to all who say that all roads lead to God.

I hope that I have been able to show that Christianity has bases in truth. Why then are people often hesitant to become Christians? I believe it is because of the consequences and fundamental change that will inevitably take place on conversion. G.K. Chesterton, the famous British Christian said, *"The Christian ideal has not been tried and found wanting. It has been found difficult and left untried."* God is a jealous God and will not share you with other idols, such as the love of money. To some, becoming a Christian would mean separation from their family and their culture. Being shunned and shamed for abandoning their original belief system. Two famous former Muslims that made this difficult transition are Abdul Murray and Nabeel Qureshi. They both acknowledged that the biggest barrier to becoming a Christian was not that there was insufficient evidence that Jesus was who He said He was, proving His deity by rising from the dead but the stigma and shame they would face from their family kept them from taking the first steps to becoming a Christian. It is not easy for us in the West to understand what a massive step conversion is for a Muslim, as we do not have an honour shame culture at the core of our society. Part of the reason that the conversion of the early Jews to Christianity is so miraculous is that they shared this honour shame culture. For devout Jews to change their worldview would have been earth-shattering and would not have been done lightly. I believe this is evidence that they did so because they saw the risen Jesus.

I have often spoken with atheists who are happy with the concept of gods with a small g but not a God with a big G. I have always found this fascinating. I think it ultimately stems from people not wanting to believe in an all-powerful, all-knowing God. If God with a small g can be kept in a box and only brought out at church or in the privacy of a believer's home, then all is well and dandy. That all-knowing, all-powerful God is a different prospect. I guess because non-believers want to keep their approach to taxes, sex, hatred, and money. They do not want to think that there are eternal consequences to their actions. I can sympathise because, as a nominal Christian, I wanted a pocket-sized God that I could take out on the occasional trip to church, feel self-righteous about the "sacrifice" I had made by getting up early on a Sunday morning and making all that effort. Looking back, I cringe at my hypocrisy.

Fallen humanity has essentially the same desires as Adam and Eve, who listened to the Devil in the Garden of Eden. The Devil promised they would become like God if they ate from the tree. We do not want another God to take our place as gods. We are blind to the mess we have made of the earth. Christianity understands that we are morally bankrupt, and no amount of going to church or charitable acts will change this. A newspaper reporter asked G. K. Chesterton to comment on what is wrong with the world. He wrote: -

Dear Sirs:
I am.
Yours Sincerely
G. K. Chesterton

Saint Paul echoed these sentiments when he said in 1 Timothy 1:15, *"Christ Jesus came into the world to save sinners, among whom I am foremost."* Was Saint Paul the worst of all sinners? No, but a Christian must understand that he is lost and needs saving from his sinful nature, not worthless. If we were worthless, Jesus would not have died for us. The value of something can be determined by what someone is prepared to pay for it. Jesus values us highly because He suffered and died so we could be redeemed.

In the world, it does not matter which famous King, Queen, pop star or president you meet, it will not change you, but if you meet with Christ, it cannot help but change you. You may carry on sinning because *"the flesh is weak,"* Matthew 26:41, but you no longer want to sin *"For the good that I want, I do not do, but I practice the very evil that I do not want,"* Roman 7:19.

Jesus' last commandment on earth should be our first priority. Mark 16:15, *"And He said to them."* Go into all the world and preach *the gospel to every creature."* If you do not desire this great commission, if it does not move you to see people you love unsaved, you must doubt your salvation.

Being a Christian is not falling but admitting it when you do.

Being a Christian is not having it all together but following the One who does!

Being a Christian is not praying a prayer or deciding for Christ; it is being under new management. Do you still hate? If so, does it bother you? Jesus said hate is like murder.

Being a Christian is putting up a thumb, not a finger, during road rage.

Being a Christian is when someone looks at you, do they think God is optional or essential in your life?

"You have one business on earth – to save souls."—John Wesley

"The Great Commission is too big for anyone to accomplish alone and too important not to try to do together."—Steve Moore

Who made fishermen fishers of men?
Who made Pilot's wife terrified about a dream?
Who made Caiaphas so mad that he tore his clothes?
Who made the dead and the lame walk?
Who made the death talk?
Who made the blind see?
Who made the Pharisees seethe?
Who made the money changers mad?
Who made the sad glad?
Who? My King, my Saviour!

If you ask a nominal Christian why they are a Christian, they may say something like they heard a good sermon or were born into that faith. That describes HOW they became a Christian, not WHY. The why question must be that Christians know that they are not good enough to be in God's presence on their merit and need a saviour to take away their sin. That is why a Christian is eternally grateful to God's all-sufficient sacrifice on a Christian's behalf.

"I am a Christian. He who answers thus has declared everything at once-his country, profession, family; the believer belongs to no city on earth but to the heavenly Jerusalem." John Chrysostom

I believe there are ten major elements to the Christian life that you need to understand the significance. These are belief, faith, compassion, denying self, repentance, forgiveness, money, love, redemption and finally, the second coming of Jesus. All these principles need to be understood how they fit into the Christians life. The following pages try to articulate each of these points in turn.

Belief

Mark 16:16, "The one who has believed and has been baptized will be saved."

> *"I believe in Christianity as I believe that the sun has risen: not only because I see it, but because by it I see everything else." C S Lewis*

Belief is defined in the Collins English dictionary as *"A principle, etc, acceptance as true."* Is belief in a God that you cannot see delusional? There are only two answers to that question. Either there is a God, and He created everything, or there is not. An argument that atheists often raise for not believing in God is why there is not more evidence of God's existence? That is a good question and worthy of an answer. The answer to this question really depends on your definition of evidence. If we look around the wonders of the universe, the fine-tuning, why there is something rather than nothing, clearly something very out of the ordinary happened at the beginning of time.

The secular world has traditionally believed in the Big Bang Theory, where everything appeared in a split second, from nothing, I may add. Even this theory is now under review. The new theory is that the universe took a lot longer to form, rather than in a split second. It seems that there is considerable doubt in the secular world as to the origins of the universe. Why is there not even more compelling evidence? Could God have written across the sky, *"I am the Lord your God"?* Isaiah 41:13. Firstly, he has, in effect, done that by the wonders in the universe. Secondly, I believe that would compel a person to believe rather than change their life because they want to love and be loved by the God of creation.

Is a belief in God delusional as many in the world would have us believe, or is it the most reasonable explanation for our existence? Proverbs 25:2 says, *"It is the glory of God to conceal a matter, But the glory of kings is to search out a matter."* Blaise Pascal said *"Belief is a wise wager. Granted that faith cannot be proved, what harm will come to you if you gamble on its truth and it proves false? If you gain, you gain all; if you lose, you lose nothing. Wager, then, without hesitation, that He exists."*

From a Christian perspective, is a belief in God all that is needed? Is belief in God all that changes a person's heart? The truth is that even if Jesus appeared in front of the most sceptical atheist and let them put their hand through His pierced side, would they repent of their ways? The Bible is full of people that walked with God and rebelled, for example, Adam and Eve. Before them, a third of the angels rebelled against God to populate hell. There are no demons in hell that do not believe in God. How do I know that? The demon-possessed man said, *"What business do You have with us, Son of God? Have You come here to torment us before the time?"* Matthew 8:29. This shows that demons believe in God. They also know scripture because the demon said, *"Have You come here to torment us before the time?"* Demons know the Bible and that ultimately, they will be cast in the lake of fire. There is no demon in hell who does not believe more than the most passionate Christian. Is it belief in God that is all-important? James 2:19 says, *"You believe that God is one. Good! Even the demons believe—and they shudder."* So, what separates us from the devils? In a word, repentance: from the Greek word "metanoia" (Μετάνοια), which means a change of mind. What do we need to change our mind about? It is to remove the idols in our life. Idols are anything that keeps us from God. We will not stop sinning, but repentance is no longer wanting to sin. In the world, millions embraced the knowledge of the gospel but show no evidence of a changed heart and life. Jesus said to Nicodemus in John 3:3, *"Truly, truly, I say to you, unless someone is born again he cannot see the kingdom of God."* The inference is that evidence of repentance is a change in your life.

People say to me, *"How can you believe in God if you don't understand everything about him?"* That is easy. After over 30 years of marriage, I do not understand everything about my wife, but she exists! It makes my relationship with my wife so unique that I am still getting to know her, making my love grow deeper. It is the same with God. I get to know him more and more through his word. If I do not fully understand one of his creations that I have spent so long with, how can I expect to know everything about the one who created her? John Chrysostom said, *"A comprehended god is no god."* Jesus marvelled twice in the Bible. Once at the Jews unbelief, Mark 6:6, and once at the gentile centurion's belief, Luke 7:9. Do you want Jesus to marvel at your unbelief or belief? Rick Warren says, *"Doubt your doubts and believe your beliefs."*

Some say that belief in God is enough. Clearly, this is not the case. As stated above, even the devils *"believe and tremble."* Coupled with believing in the existence of God, a Christian needs to have faith from the Greek word "pisti" (Πίστη), which is to trust God.

Faith

Hebrews 11:1, "Now faith is the certainty of things hoped for, a proof of things not seen."

> *"In faith there is enough light for those who want to believe and enough shadows to blind those who don't."*
> *Blaise Pascal*

The secular world believes that faith in God is believing in something that is not true, just like the tooth fairy or unicorns. It is perceived that the more faith a person has, the more confident they are that what they believe is not true. The world looks at Christians and sees them as content, different from the rest of society. You can almost sense the pity in them that a Christian believes in something (God) that is non-existent but can see the effect on a Christian's life in that they are happy in their delusion. People will often talk about blind faith, saying that Christians accept the Bible with no evidence. That is not what Christianity is; Christianity invites questions. When one of Jesus' disciples, Thomas, heard of the resurrection of Jesus, he said, *"Unless I see in His hands the imprint of the nails, and put my finger into the place of the nails, and put my hand into His side, I will not believe."* John 20:25. Christianity takes on difficult questions and does not expect acceptance (blind faith) without answering life's toughest challenges. That is a critical test of Christianity that it can answer those tough questions and offer comfort.

I remember having a debate with an atheist. He quoted an argument used quite often of the "invisible dragon in the garage." The argument essentially is if you are told of an invisible dragon in the garage, why would you believe it? Christianity is thought of in the same terms as the invisible dragon. My response was he was right if there was no evidence to believe in the dragon, then why would I believe in it? On the other hand, if I knew the garage was locked with no way in or out but on the wall, I saw the words, *"I am an invisible dragon and live in a garage"* mysteriously appeared. Then I would have evidence that something out of the ordinary had happened which warrants an explanation. In the same way, the Christian asks questions that need answering. Jesus' empty tomb, the conversion of the sceptical followers of Jesus into martyrs and the marvels of the universe all need an explanation which a Christian believes are provided in the Bible. The Greek word for faith is "pisti" (Πίστη), which more accurately translated as "to be persuaded." A Christian is persuaded that his worldview explains the origins of our existence, how to live, why we are here and where we go after the test of life.

Sigmund Freud, the psychologist said that belief in God is a way for people dealing with life. So, the view from Atheism is that faith in God is like a comfort blanket. However, if God exists, then it is the atheist who is after the comfort blanket, as they do not want to believe in being held accountable for their wrongdoing. Psychological studies show that true believers are generally physically and mentally fitter than those who are not. Not because of some kind of magic that being a Christian brings in and of itself. It is the fact that Christians are at peace with God, knowing that even death is not the end. Saint Peter, faced with prison and worse, was sleeping soundly when the angel came to release him from prison. The angel had to wake him from his slumber. Such was Saint Peters confidence in God, Acts 12:7. *"Faith never knows where it is being led, but it loves and knows the One who is leading." – Oswald Chambers.*

If you have small faith, like a small flame, the wind comes and blows the flame out. When you have a large faith, the wind comes and fans the flame into a large flame.

Without faith, it is impossible to please God. What does this mean exactly? An example would be if you promised your child that you would support them through university, but they said, *"Dad I don't trust or have faith that you will do this, so transfer the money to my account now."* It would be heartbreaking for a parent to hear this. It is the same when we do not have faith in God's promises.

Often people will lose their faith or reject Christianity based on a bad experience at Church or less than exemplary behaviour from the clergy. Jesus predicted this in Matthew 7:21, *"Not everyone who says to Me, 'Lord, Lord,' will enter the kingdom of heaven, but he who does the will of My Father who is in heaven will enter."* I remember seeing in a monastery of devout monks an icon that portrays the parable of the rich young ruler, Mark 10:17-31. The icon shows a narrow gate as the entrance to heaven and a wide gate to hell. Priests were entering the wide and the narrow gate, acknowledging that not all clergy are worthy of a place in heaven. In the same way, we would not stop using banks because of a bad experience. You simply find a good bank.

We cannot be saved by any number of good works that we may do, but if our "faith" does not produce good works after we are saved, that will prove that our faith is not genuine. *"Faith without (good) works is dead."* James 2:26. Faith needs a backbone, not a wishbone.

> *"Faith does not eliminate questions. But*
> *faith knows where to take them."*
> *Elisabeth Elliot*

Once a Christian develops faith and trusts Christ, we will want to emulate Jesus and display compassion to our fellow man.

Compassion

Matthew 14:14 *"When He came ashore, He saw a large crowd, and felt compassion for them and healed their sick."*

> *"When you are weary of praying, and do not receive,*
> *consider how often you have heard a poor man calling,*
> *and have not listened to him."*

John Chrysostom

The Collins English dictionary defines compassion as, *"a feeling of distress and pity for the suffering or misfortune of another."* If you feel sorry for your neighbour, you are moralising. If you do something about their plight, you have compassion. It is easy for us to moralise. We get upset when we see the poor of this world suffering, some dying slowly through starvation. In contrast, the people in Western societies die of "rich man's diseases," including obesity, heart disease, to name a few. We may toss a few coins to our favourite charity on occasion to ease our conscience, but how many of us are prepared to make a real difference? Compassion costs! It will cost you your time, your money, your energy. How many of us are prepared to pay? When watching the suffering in the media, it is easier to change the channel than to change our heart and the priorities of our lives to help those in need.

Compassion is easy if you can imagine what it is like to be in the shoes of another person suffering, but most of us like the shoes we are wearing. They fit so comfortably, whereas the sufferer's shoes look uncomfortable. Many of us like the idea of being compassionate while warming our feet by the fire, but to get up and go into the cold and find someone that needs our help that is undoubtedly someone else's job. We say to ourselves, *"I am not equipped for that; besides, it is so nice and warm by this fireplace."* Or we make excuses for ourselves, saying, *"well, I just need to finish my studies, or get married, or buy my first house, or raise my children or save for my retirement, or need to provide for my funeral."* The mother of all excuses is, *"charity begins at home."* There is always a good reason to put things off for tomorrow, but there is a better reason to be compassionate today. Thomas Aquinas said, *"I would rather feel compassion than know the meaning of it."* Compassion is only compassion if it costs you. Jesus highlighted this principle in Luke 21:1-4, which is the story of the Widow's gift, *"Now He looked up and saw the wealthy putting their gifts into the temple treasury. And He saw a poor widow putting in two lepta coins. And He said, "Truly I say to you, this poor widow put in more than all of them; for they all contributed to the offering from their surplus; but she, from her poverty, put in all that she had to live on."* Jesus was moved by the suffering he saw and would cure the sick and the lame. More importantly, he was moved by compassion because of their spiritual emptiness as the religious leaders were leading them astray. Mark 6:34, *"When Jesus went ashore, He saw a large crowd, and He felt compassion for them because they were like sheep without a shepherd; and He began to teach them many things."* Of course, the greatest act of compassion that Jesus has given the world is in giving His life as a ransom for us. John 3:16, *"For God so loved the world, that He gave His only Son, so that everyone who believes in Him will not perish, but have eternal life."*

"God keeps all our tears in a bottle; so precious is the water that is distilled from penitent eyes; and because he will be sure not to fail, he notes how many drops there be in his register. It was a precious ointment wherewith the woman in the Pharisee's house (it is thought Mary Magdalene) anointed the feet of Christ; but her tears, wherewith she washed them, were more worth than her spikenard." Abraham Wright

Denying self

Mattew 16:24, Then Jesus said to His disciples, "If anyone wishes to come after Me, he must deny himself, and take up his cross and follow Me."

"The most important qualification for a servant of God is that he does not seek his own." Zac Poonen

Self-denial is a fundamental element of Christian living. It is the driving force behind Christians traveling the world over, working in

NGO's (non-government organisations) giving their time and money to promote those in need in war-torn and famine-stricken areas at the expense of their self-interests. It should be a desire in every Christian's life to have a sense of compassion. To be a Christian is to follow Christ in his self-denial. The most remarkable example of this is in the garden of Gethsemane. Jesus anguished over the pending physical pain and spiritual separation from God. In Luke 22:42, he cried out *"Father, if You are willing, remove this cup from Me; yet not My will, but Yours be done."* Most of us read this and think Jesus does not want to go through the crucifixion's physical pain. That is not the prime reason Jesus is partitioning God. Jesus' anguish is because he knew that God would have to break fellowship with Him when He became sin for humanity. This was an unimaginable torment that caused Jesus to sweat blood literally, Luke 22:44. The anguish is based on the intense love that the Trinity has for each other. Whilst most Christians try to understand the price Jesus paid on the cross, we often forget the Father's agony, having lost the fellowship of His Son. If you meet a person who has buried a child, you get a small insight into how traumatic that experience is for them, and so what God had to endure. I always wonder at the love of the Trinity for creation.

It is the Christians calling to *"Love your neighbour as yourself,"* Matthew 22:39, which will invariably come at the expense of a person's self-interest. An illustration of this is in Matthew 16:24, *"Then Jesus said to His disciples, "If anyone wishes to come after Me, he must deny himself, and take up his cross and follow Me."* Following this command comes with a promise, Matthew 19:29, *"And everyone who has left houses or brothers or sisters or father or mother or children or farms for My name's sake, will receive many times as much, and will inherit eternal life."* If we believe this, nothing we give up in this short life should be considered too high a price when we contemplate what we are offered in return. While we are not to fight for our rights, we should stand up for others' rights.

*"The bee is more honoured than other animals, not because
she labours, but because she labours for others."*
John Chrysostom

*"If we do not die to ourselves, we cannot live to God,
and he that does not live to God, is dead."*
George Macdonald

*"Those who determine not to put self to death will never see
the will of God fulfilled in their lives. Those who ought to
become the light of the world must necessarily burn and become
less and less. By denying self, we are able to win others."*
Sadhu Sundar Singh

*"Bearing a cross is an elaboration of Christ's demand
for self-denial. Bearing a cross is every Christian's daily,
conscious selection of those options which will please
Christ, pain self, and aim at putting self to death."*
Walter J. Chantry

The prime motivator for self-denial is to emulate Christ and to
repent of our ways knowing our weaknesses and failings.

Repentance

**Luke 15:10, "In the same way, I tell you, there is joy in the
presence of the angels of God over one sinner who repents."**

*"Another proof of the conquest of a soul for Christ will
be found in a real change of life. If the man does not
live differently from what he did before, both at home
and abroad, his repentance needs to be repented of and
his conversion is a fiction." Charles Spurgeon*

The Collins English dictionary's definition of repentance is: *"remorse or contrition for one's past actions."* How often have you heard someone say, *"I am a good person."* The question is by whose standard? Clearly, not God's standard. Romans 3:23 says, *"For all have sinned and fall short of the glory of God."* God's standard is impossible to attain while we live in a fallen world with all its temptations. We will never measure up to God's perfect will. We can, however, turn from wilfully disobeying God. We can only see a small percentage of our faults and sins, so we should work on ensuring we no longer disobey God in the areas of our life that we can acknowledge as sinful. Incidentally, that is one of the reasons why we should not judge others. If we can only see a small part of our sinful life, how can we judge others of their wrongdoing when we know little of their life and subsequent struggles? This changing of mind is at the heart of the Christian's walk with God. It is turning away from the idols we hold dear and cause us to sin, living contrary to God's laws. An idol is not necessarily a statue of a deity; it is anything or anyone that takes God's place. It can be the love of money, a partner, a car, a house, a job. C.S. Lewis said, *"No man knows how bad he is till he has tried very hard to be good. A silly idea is current that good people do not know what temptation means. This is an obvious lie. Only those who try to resist temptation know how strong it is."* Watchman Nee said, *"People who cover their faults and excuse themselves do not have a repentant spirit."*

A repentant heart is an essential element of being a Christian. John the Baptist was sent as a herald ahead of Jesus. A herald went ahead of a king to prepare for the coming monarch, ensuring the road was fit for the king to travel and announce the king was coming. John the Baptist's principal message was to repent. To hammer home the importance of repentance, Jesus himself said in Matthew 4:17, *"Repent, for the kingdom of heaven is at hand."* Peter went on to say in Acts 2:38, *"Repent, and each of you be baptized in the name of Jesus Christ for the forgiveness of your sins; and you will receive the gift of the Holy Spirit."*

Why is it so important for a person to repent before being accepted into fellowship with God? Why can't God accept people for who they are without the need for repentance? The answer is that a Holy God cannot fellowship with those who are knowingly sinful. Jesus will not force his way into your life. He wants to have a relationship with you, but it must be a mutual relationship. A person needs to invite Jesus into their life with the assurance that Jesus will accept them, should they do so regardless of their past life. Matthew 7:8, *"For everyone who asks receives, and the one who seeks finds, and to the one who knocks it will be opened."* The Bible frequently refers to the relationship of Jesus with His church as a bridegroom with his bride. No bridegroom can force a marriage with his bride, and so the relationship must be based on mutual acceptance. Jesus is always ready to accept us, but we need to accept Him to complete the marriage. We cannot bring anything to the relationship that Jesus needs. We can only come to Him in repentance, sorry for all the times we put ourselves first instead of Him. While we will continue to sin in this world, we should turn from wilfully sinning.

The fruits of repentance are evidence of a genuinely contrite heart. Just as we have received forgiveness from God for our transgressions, we need to forgive others that have wronged us. Matthew 6:12, *"And forgive us our debts, as we also have forgiven our debtors."* The forgiveness must be personal to the individual you have wronged, not just a generic confession at church. Once forgiveness has been sought, restitution needs to follow. For example, if you have not paid your taxes, you need to pay back what you owe. If you have stolen from someone, you need to repay what is due to them. If you understand the value of the forgiveness that God offers you, in turn, will be overjoyed at the prospect of making restitution as a small token of what you have received. In Luke 19:8, it says, *"Zacchaeus stopped and said to the Lord, "Behold, Lord, half of my possessions I am giving to the poor, and if I have extorted anything from anyone, I am giving back four times as much."* Zacchaeus was so overwhelmed at being forgiven for his sins that he thought it was a small price to pay to restore all that he had cheated people over the years.

Luke 15:11 is the famous parable of the prodigal son, the parable is about the Father waiting and looking out for his disobedient son to change his ways. This is a picture of our Father in heaven waiting for us to change from our sinful habits. We need to have the attitude of the prodigal to repent of our sins Luke 15:18, *"I will set out and go to my father, and will say to him, "Father, I have sinned against heaven, and in your sight."* When others sin against us, we need to have a forgiving heart like the Father in the prodigal's story.

Many people say that God is a spoilsport wanting us to give up something good and enjoyable. Everything that God prohibits is ultimately for our good. Matthew 7:9-11, *"What person is there among you who, when his son asks for a loaf of bread, will give him a stone? Or if he asks for a fish, he will not give him a snake, will he? So if you, despite being evil, know how to give good gifts to your children, how much more will your Father who is in heaven give good things to those who ask!"*

Being repentant does not mean you will not get angry, but you will not want to be angry. It does not mean you will not lust, but you will not want to lust. This change of heart is not through fear of being punished by God but love for Him. You no longer want to grieve God but do what is pleasing to Him. In conclusion, repentance, from the Greek word "metanoia" (μετάνοια) means a changing of the mind. Changing your mind to be more like God in loving what God loves, no longer seeking your own will, but God's will.

One of the consequences of being repentant is to learn to forgive because we have been forgiven. We cannot claim to be Christians if we do not forgive others in the same way God has forgiven us.

Forgiveness

Colossians 3:13, "Bearing with one another, and forgiving each other, whoever has a complaint against anyone; just as the Lord forgave you, so also should you."

"And nothing makes us so like God, as being ready to forgive the wicked and wrongdoers; even as indeed He had taught before, when He spoke of His "making the sun to shine on the evil and the good." John Chrysostom.

The disciple Peter asks Jesus how often he should forgive someone; Peter thinks he is being generous by suggesting forgiving them seven times. Jesus replies with a ridiculously high figure (70 times 7). Jesus said this to emphasise that we should forgive without reservation and limit. As was Jesus' style, He then illustrates the principle of forgiveness by telling a parable of the unforgiving servant in Matthew 18:23-35. This parable portrays a king who is calling in his debtors. One of his debtors has a huge debt (about ten million pounds at today's rate). The king orders the servant and his family to be sold into slavery to pay back what is owed. The servant pleads with the king to give him a chance to pay back the debt. The king has compassion for the servant and wipes the debt clean. The servant then finds a fellow servant that owed him a small sum of money. He roughly treats him and demands payment in full. When the king hears of this, he is enraged that the first servant never showed mercy, just as the king showed mercy and so reinstates the first servant's debt. He is put in prison till the debt is paid in full. This parable illustrates the seriousness of, firstly not appreciating the debt that we have been forgiven (the first servant had the slate cleaned for an unpayable amount). Secondly, not forgive those who have wronged us. C.S. Lewis sums this up beautifully, *"To be a Christian means to forgive the inexcusable, because God has forgiven the inexcusable in you."* Forgiveness is a command of God. The Lord's Prayer also includes this principle of forgiveness. Therefore, we need to in the same way reciprocate that forgiveness to our fellow man. *"Forgive us our debts, as we also have forgiven our debtors."* Matthew 6:12.

Having a forgiving attitude has a practical aspect. Studies have shown that people who harbour an unforgiving attitude are more prone to suffer from mental and physical illnesses. I can personally attest to this in my life. Forgiving does not mean that you instantly trust a person. Forgiving deals with the past and is instant; trust deals with the future and is earned. Someone that was abused should forgive the abuser but not trust them until they have earned that trust once more. God forgives us without remembering our sins, *"For I will be merciful toward their wrongdoings, and their sins I will no longer remember."* Hebrews 8:12. We need to forgive in the same way. On a similar theme Thomas Fuller says, *"He that cannot forgive others breaks the bridge over which he must pass himself; for every man has need to be forgiven."*

Most people are happy with the idea of forgiveness if the guy next door is doing the forgiving. When we need to do the forgiving, we come up with all kinds of reasons we should not forgive. *"You don't know what they did to me"* or *"that's easy for you to forgive, but they hurt me."* The list is endless, and I am sure you can add dozens of scenarios. However, what has happened to you or me pales into insignificance when we consider the miscarriage of justice that led Jesus on the long road to Golgotha, carrying the instrument of his death on his back and dying slowly and painfully. More importantly, breaking fellowship with His Father for the first and only time in eternity. What did Jesus say when faced with this undeserved travesty of justice? *"Father, forgive them; for they do not know what they are doing."* Luke 23:34. Can any of us dare to compare what has happened to us with what Jesus endured for his creation?

Have you noticed many family arguments, and indeed the world's problems have money as the root cause? Money is one of the main reasons that tensions occur in marriages, societies and between nations.

Money

Ecclesiastes 5:10, "One who loves money will not be satisfied with money"

> "A dreadful thing is the love of money! It disables both eyes and ears, and makes men worse to deal with than a wild beast, allowing a man to consider neither conscience nor friendship nor fellowship nor salvation."
> John Chrysostom

Perhaps surprisingly, Jesus spoke frequently about money. Why? In Jesus' own words, he said in Matthew 6:21, "For where your treasure is, there your heart will be also." Money is a projection of what you believe to be important to you in your life. You can tell where a person's heart is by looking at their bank statements to see where they spend their money and time. Do you spend your money and your energy to do Gods will or your will? The story of Zacchaeus, Luke 19:1-10, showed when he came to faith, it changed his heart and how he used his money. He had previously cheated people of their money, abusing his position as a tax collector. Once he came to faith, he repaid those that he had cheated.

We all need money to live, but we need to put our wealth in its rightful place as money is a good servant but a terrible master. Luke 16:13, "No servant can serve two masters; for either he will hate the one and love the other, or he will be devoted to one and despise the other. You cannot serve God and wealth." God does not need your money but giving to God is pleasing to Him as it shows you trust Him and not your wealth.

In Matthew 8:33, Jesus heals a demoniac by allowing the demons that had previously possessed the man to go into a herd of pigs that rush into the lake and drown. The herdsmen looking after the pigs had witnessed an amazing miracle, but instead of rejoicing that the demon-possessed man was in his right mind, they asked Jesus to leave. Why? It would seem they would rather have the man possessed by demons rather than lose the pigs and, by extension, their wealth. They valued money more than man, a common theme in the world.

As was their practice, the Pharisees laid a trap for Jesus and asked, should they pay taxes to Caesar? Jesus answered, *"Pay to Caesar the things that are Caesar's, and to God the things that are God's."* Mark 12:17. Ravi Zacharias joked that whenever he fills in his tax return, he wishes Jesus would have answered this question differently. The essence of Jesus' answer to the Pharisees is that we should not be above the government despite being Christians. The only exception is when the government's laws are contrary to God's laws. It is not a sin to be rich, but it is a sin not to give thanks for what God has given you.

Jesus acknowledged that being wealthy makes being righteous more challenging as money can take the place of God. Jesus said to the rich young ruler, *"It is easier for a camel to go through the eye of a needle, than for a rich person to enter the kingdom of God,"* Mark 10:25. The rich young ruler's error was not in his wealth but in loving his possessions more than his neighbour. 1 Timothy 6:10 says, *"For the love of money is the root of all sorts of evil."* Money itself is not evil or good. However, money can make a person proud that they could attain great wealth, rather than the realisation that God has given them the ability to gain money by God-given talents or circumstance. Examples of this could be from a rich parent or your abilities as a musician, sports personality, artist, etc.

While money has no morality in and of itself, money is a measure of morality by what you spend it on. In the Old Testament, believers were mandated to give 10% of their income to the needy as rules and regulations were in place to govern charitable donations. In the New Testament, there are no rules or regulations on giving. Each believer is led to give what they have searched their heart for. In 2 Corinthians 8, it says, *"For I testify that according to their ability, and beyond their ability, they gave voluntarily."* Mother Terresa always maintained that any charitable donation must affect your circumstance for the contribution to be of real value. Giving to the needy should be for the right motive, not to ease your conscience or for pity but love for the one in need.

For most of human history the average person had barely enough money and wealth to subsist. Humankind never had lifestyle choices. The modern era is the first time in history that we have advertising. The purpose of advertising is a scheme to separate you from your money, to buy things we do not need, to impress people we do not really like. Advertising tells us that we need to be more beautiful, younger-looking, conform to an unobtainable image, be better travelled, and have a lovely house. Most of us in the west have nothing we need but lots of things we want. It was once said, *"The world is big enough for every man's needs but not big enough for one man's greed."* These "wants" fill the place of our true need, and that is to have harmony with our creator. We have more disposable income than our parents and grandparents, but we have more financial problems than them, thanks to advertising. As a result, this has led to a massive increase in divorce. Eighty per cent of couples site financial worries as the main reason for the breakup.

Some Christians believe that we should have just enough wealth to survive. Looking at the wonders of the world, I do not think that is the case. Why would God have gone to all the trouble of making all the wonderful foods if we could have just basic food that meets our physiological needs but was bland to eat? Why are there so many beautiful gems, diamonds, gold, etc? We are biblically expected to gain wealth. The Bible is very explicit as it says in 2 Thessalonians 3:10, *"If anyone is not willing to work, then he is not to eat, either."* Again, in Proverbs 6:6 it says, *"Go to the ant, you lazy one, Observe its ways and be wise."* Clearly, we are expected to work. We cannot achieve wealth by stealing it, exploiting others to gain it, defrauding people of money, or gamble for it. The crime is not in wealth but in thinking your wealth makes you better than another person. We are commanded to *"love our neighbour as ourselves."* That command will invariably lead to acts of charity. *"The rich man is not one who is in possession of much, but one who gives much." John Chrysostom.*

The fact that we have wealth is temporal. In the final analysis, Earth will be destroyed, much less the wealth a person accumulates in a lifetime. The parable of the rich fool in Luke 12:20 speaks to this. The rich fool has a bumper harvest and plans on taking it easy for the rest of his life. God, however, has other ideas when he says, *"You fool! This very night your soul is demanded of you; and as for all that you have prepared, who will own it now?"*

Where we spend our money shows who and what we love. Do we spend money on ourselves or others?

Love

1 John 4:8, "The one who does not love does not know God, because God is love."

"Human things must be known to be loved; but Divine things must be loved to be known." Blaise Pascal

What is Love? Love is one of Google's top searches; clearly, it is an important question that people want answers for. Love has been the topic of writers, poets, and philosophers for as long as humans have been able to express themselves through the medium of writing. The English language is deficient when it comes to the word "love." You can love your friend, car, chocolate milkshake and your spouse. The same word is used in all these instances. In Greek, there are four words to describe what we call love in English, Eros, (romantic love), Phileo, (enjoyment, fondness, friendship), Storge (family loyalty) and Agape (unconditional love, unconcerned with the self and concerned with the greatest good of another). Agape is the love that gives but never takes. It is the kind of love that seeks the highest good for another, no matter its cost.

I have been blessed with amazing parents. They worked long hours in the fish and chip shop to make sure my sisters and I had all we needed. The house and my siblings and I were always spotlessly clean. My parents, despite their exhaustion, would invariably take us to meet friends and family at the weekends or a place of interest. The beach at Margate was a favourite as well as the local parks. The greatest gift my parents gave us only became apparent in the later years. An example to us of true love. My parents were not the romantic type. It is common to associate romantic gestures with love. However, showering your partner with gifts could be for selfish reasons, as you may hope your partner cooks you your favourite meal or something else for your pleasure. My parents were not big on romantic gestures. They seldom went to hotels for the weekends to celebrate anniversaries or birthdays. I only remember one occasion when my father sent my mother flowers. Their love was so much deeper than that. It was the kind of self-sacrificing love that always gives without expecting anything in return. They would always fight over who would do the extended shifts in the shop so the other could rest. They worked together and spent almost all their time in each other's company which is only possible in a strong relationship.

My mother started showing signs of a degenerative brain disorder in her later years. She was less and less capable of everyday tasks. My father started doing more and more for her expecting nothing in return. It is a heartbreaking sight to watch such a hardworking person, like my mother, slowly degenerating. I think the greatest example of their love was when my mother broke her hip in 2018. My mother was rushed to hospital, eventually ending up in an intensive therapy unit. She was unconscious most of the time. Despite this, my father would make two trips to the hospital every day during visiting times. He would drive 100 kilometres a day in the summer heat to be by my mothers' side only to watch her in a deep sleep, unable to communicate with him. He would cry repeatedly and reminisce about the life they had together. There was nothing my father would not do for my mother in those final days. Unfortunately, after 73 days of fighting for her life, she took a turn for the worse on the 14th of September 2018. The doctors said they needed to operate on her to try and save her life but gave her little chance of surviving the surgery. The doctors explained this to my father, and a consent form was given to him to sign. He knew that the chances of survival were minimal, but he also knew that her passing would be a merciful release for her. My father told the doctor that he signed the consent form because of his great love for my mother. I will never forget this; it was my parents' most incredible gift, to show me the love that always gives but never takes. I hope and pray that I can emulate this intense love that my parents had for each other.

I think this is the closest example that I have personally come across to God's love for us. God showed His agape by giving us His only Son, *"For God so loved the world, that He gave His only begotten Son, that whoever believes in Him shall not perish, but have eternal life,"* John 3:16. Jesus said, *"Greater love has no one than this, that a person will lay down his life for his friends."* John 15:13. What kept Jesus fastened to the cross? It was not the nails, but his love for humanity! Agape is unconquerable benevolence and invincible goodness; it is entirely selfless.

When I first got to know my wife, I was so in love, but all my older friends and family told me that what I felt was nothing to the love I would feel after knowing her for a while. I thought these people could not really love their partners, as I thought I could not love my wife anymore. Now the years have rolled by, and I realise that what I felt was eros (romantic love) and now understand more of what agape love is.

The words "I love you" are only significant if the person that says them truly knows you, your shortcomings, failings, and bad habits, as well as the good stuff. True love is not the absence of judgment; it is the presence of judgment. You cannot say you love someone without knowing them, which means you know their faults too. When God says he loves us, he knows everything about us, our weaknesses and inadequacies, everything we have done wrong and everything we will do wrong. That is what makes His love truly meaningful! Compassion is when you make a moral judgement about something and are moved to do something about it. If you do not do anything about it, you are moralising. God looks at the human condition and is moved to do something about it. That is the cross! That is where God's love, judgment, and compassion come together on the cross of Jesus Christ. Most people do not have anyone in their lives who loves them enough to tell them the truth, even when it means they will continue in self-destructive ways. You cannot rebuke people strongly unless you love them. When James and John were seeking places of honour, Jesus rebuked them. When they wanted to call down fire on the Samaritans, He rebuked them. He rebuked His disciples seven times for unbelief. Why? - Because He loved them. If He did not care for them, Jesus would not have corrected them. Only true love can have the courage to rebuke and correct.

The laws on love:
The best use of life is love.
The best expression of love is your time.
The best time to love is now.

You show how much you love someone by how much time you spend with them. Time is the one thing you cannot make more of. Why do people watch other people's families on reality TV shows rather than working on their own family's reality? Why do people spend time watching repeats of "Friends" instead of making friends? Love is an action; you choose to love; Love does not happen by accident. That is infatuation. Love is making someone else's agenda your agenda.

Why did God not take us straight to heaven when we became Christians? We are on earth to learn to love. We do not take anything else to heaven but our character. When you go to heaven, God will ask "did you do the two things I asked you to do? Love Me and love your neighbour?"

Jesus said that if you cannot love your brother that you have seen, how can you love God that you have not seen? Jesus was tried, beaten, scourged, and put to death for being the Messiah, the Christ, the anointed one. He could have called legions of angels to fight for Him. Though He was guiltless and did nothing wrong, Jesus did the loving thing and died for the world. Sometimes you need to be loving rather than fight for your rights.

Quotes on love

"The love of husband and wife is the force that welds society together." John Chrysostom
"When you give someone your time, you are giving them a portion of your life that you'll never get back. Your time is your life. That is why the greatest gift you can give someone is your time"
Rick Warren.

"Generosity is impossible apart from our love of God and of His people. But with such love, generosity not only is possible but inevitable"
John MacArthur

"Love is larger than the walls which shut it in."
Corrie Ten Boom

"You will never really love until you love someone who hates you."
Jack Hayles

"You can always give without loving, but you can never love without giving." Amy Carmichael

"There is nothing you can do that will make God stop loving you. You could try, but you simply can't do it - because his love for you is based upon his character and not on anything you do or say or feel"
Rick Warren

"Unconditional love is an illogical notion, but such a great and powerful one." A.J. Jacobs

The ultimate love story is the cross, where Jesus took on the sins of the world to redeem his creation.

Redemption – Jesus is the way

Luke 9:22 *"The Son of Man must suffer many things and be rejected by the elders and chief priests and scribes, and be killed and be raised on the third day."*

"We live and die; Christ died and lived!" John Stott

It is common for people to imagine a god that fits their worldview. How often have you heard someone say I like to think of god as a bearded grandfather or some other image that they feel comfortable with. In today's western society, it seems that we are to believe that all roads lead to God. It does not matter which road you take; all will lead to God in the long run. This view is at odds with Jesus. Jesus said, *"I am the way, and the truth, and the life; no one comes to the Father except through Me."* John 14:6. Many claim that Christianity is an arrogant religion because it preaches exclusivity. This statement by Jesus is indeed exclusive, but is it arrogant? It cannot be arrogant if it is the truth. It is a bit like saying gravity is arrogant because it claims to be the force that attracts a body to the earth's centre. Was Jesus just a good man and an inspirational teacher or was he who he claimed to be, God incarnate? In Matthew 26:63, the high priest

Caiaphas says, *"I place You under oath by the living God, to tell us whether You are the Christ, the Son of God." Jesus said to him, "You have said it yourself. But I tell you, from now on you will see the Son of Man sitting at the right hand of power, and coming on the clouds of heaven."* In some mental health hospitals, some patients claim to be God. Was Jesus another of these people? As previously discussed, there is lots of historical evidence that points to Jesus being raised from the dead, proving He is the son of God. 1 Corinthians 15:13-14 says, *"But if there is no resurrection of the dead, then not even Christ has been raised; and if Christ has not been raised, then our preaching is in vain, your faith also is in vain."*

No matter what religion you believe in, sin is serious, and the perpetrator needs to be accountable. The only way a holy God can punish sin is not by giving you sickness or financial ruin; it is by cutting you off from Him as evil cannot dwell with a holy God. When a person is born, they are indoctrinated into the religion they are born into. Every person is born with a conscience no matter what religion they follow. When they tell a lie, their conscience convicts them. As children grow older, they learn to suppress their conscience after they have been taught that lying is not serious; they can then tell a lie without giving it away in their appearance. This does not mean that sin has become less serious, but that we humans belittle sin and excuse it away by saying that everyone is doing it. For example: Stealing from their employer, having adulterous relationships, cheating on their taxes. We belittle sin to the point that we no longer call it sin, which helps ease our conscience. We call stealing from our employer pilfering, adultery we call sleeping around and cheating on our tax's we call tax evasion.

Some people say why is God not like my mum, who forgives me when I break a plate? If sin were as trivial as breaking a plate, He would forgive us, but God, if He is just, cannot let sin go unpunished just as we are indignant when we see injustice. If we hear of paedophiles, we want them punished. If we hear of heinous murder cases, we want the perpetrator punished. However, when it comes to our deeds, we want to be excused saying, *"you don't understand what I have gone through,"* or *"if only you knew why I did it."* These double standards of ours are not God's standards. God must judge us in righteousness.

God, however, has made a way to pay for our sins. A picture of this is if a son commits a crime and the just punishment is a million-pound fine, he goes before the judge who happens to be his father. The judge cannot simply excuse the son of the fine as the judge would be branded unjust and corrupt, so he says to the son he has to pay the fine in full. The son, however, has no money to pay the fine. The judge takes off his judge's robes and writes a cheque to pay the son's fine. This is a picture of Jesus' redemptive work on the cross. There is only one thing the son must do; it is accepting the money. Being a Christian, in simple terms, is knowing we are debtors and have no means to pay, but we accept what Jesus has done as full payment for our wrongdoing. There is no other religion that claims that their saviour is God's son and born of a virgin. No other religion claims that their leader died for the world's sins, and no other leader has risen from the dead. People who have risen from the dead have credibility, so you should note what they have to say! All other religions base salvation on works, that is trying to be good.

In the Christian worldview, a person acknowledges that they can never be good enough to measure up to God's perfect will. In our fallen state, Jesus redeems us through the cross. Is the cross an extravagant over-engineered process? A legitimate question. Even Jesus asked this question just before he was to be led away to crucifixion. In Luke 42:22, Jesus says, *"Father, if You are willing, remove this cup from Me."* Was the cross necessary? If you understand how grave sin is and if you believe in a righteous God, not a God who "winks" at our sin but who loves us enough to die on the cross for us, then it is the only way a path can be made for fallen man to be redeemed and to restore fellowship for eternity.

Jesus did not come to make bad people good but to make dead people live.

Why was Jesus crucified? Not for Judas' greed, not for Pilot in fear, not for the Jews for envy but for the Father for love.

The second coming of Christ

Acts 1:10-11 "And as they were gazing intently into the sky while He was going, then behold, two men in white clothing stood beside them, and they said, "Men of Galilee, why do you stand looking into the sky? This Jesus, who has been taken up from you into heaven, will come in the same way as you have watched Him go into heaven."

> *"For this time it will be God without disguise; something so overwhelming that it will strike either irresistible love or irresistible horror into every creature. It will be too late then to choose your side." C. S. Lewis*

We live in times unprecedented in human history. Man is destroying the environment at an alarming rate, turning lush vegetation into deserts. Famine is spreading, and COVID-19 has been blamed on man's encroachment into the animal kingdom. We are using up the earth's resources disproportionate to our needs. Thanks to technology and social media, we are more connected than ever, but loneliness is common. The nuclear powers boast of their ability to destroy the earth multiple times; I think that once is enough. It seems that everyone agrees that the world needs "fixing." There is, however, no consensus on the solution. The political view of the left-wing parties believes more state involvement is the answer, in contrast, the right-wing parties desire less government control. Some say more laws, others less. The opinions are endless. If we cannot agree on what is wrong with the world, how can we mere mortals fix it? It would seem logical for God to want to intervene and change what is happening here on earth. If you rented out your house and came to find the tenants had damaged your property, you would evict them. Surely God will do the same? In Mark 12 1-9, the Parable of the Tenant portrays the world as a vineyard. God is the owner; the tenants are the inhabitants of the world. The owner (God) tries everything to get his due rent; finally, he sends his son (a picture of Jesus), who is killed. The owner runs out of patience. The final sentence in this parable is: *"What will the owner of the vineyard do? He will come and put the vine-growers to death, and give the vineyard to others."*

One of the controversial elements of the Christian life is the return of Christ, His second appearance. Many today do not believe in the second coming of Christ (including some Christians) and ridicule those who believe in Jesus' return. In 2 Peter 3:3-4 it says, *"In the last days mockers will come with their mocking, following after their own lusts, and saying, "Where is the promise of His coming?"* Why is this such a disputed issue when the Bible has so many references to this event, just like Jesus' first appearance? In fact, there are more references to the second coming than the first. Of the 46 Old Testament prophets, less than 10 of them speak of Jesus first coming, 36 of His second coming. The second coming is a central theme of the Bible, so there is no basis for not accepting it.

The reasons for the second coming are; God promised it in scripture, *"I am coming quickly"* Revelation 3:11. And so, the credibility of the triune God is at stake. Throughout the New Testament, the Holy Spirit, claims that Jesus is going to return. The apostle Paul, James, John, Peter, Jude – all wrote in the New Testament's Epistles predicting the appearance of Jesus Christ on earth for a second time. What exactly is the second coming of Christ? It is the time when Jesus will physically return to earth, setting up His kingdom, the time in the Bible which covers the rapture to the end of the kingdom age.

To fulfil Gods promises, as mentioned earlier, there are numerous references to this event throughout the Bible. The first time Jesus came to earth 2000 years ago, He fulfilled Old Testament prophecies. For example, Isaiah 7:14 says, *"Behold, the virgin will conceive."* He was indeed born of a virgin. Micah 5:2 predicted Jesus' place of birth, *"But as for you, Bethlehem Ephrathah, Too little to be among the clans of Judah, From you One will come forth for Me to be ruler in Israel."* Jesus was born in Bethlehem, despite it not being his hometown. Betrayed by a friend as predicted in Psalm 41:9 *"Even my close friend in whom I trusted, Who ate my bread, Has lifted up his heel against me".* Jesus was betrayed for thirty pieces of silver Zechariah 11:12, *"So they weighed out thirty shekels of silver as my wages."* It was one of his inner circle, Judas, a trusted disciple who betrayed Him. Psalm 22:16 says, *"They pierced my hands and my feet."* The resurrected Jesus later showed the marks made by the nails to Thomas when he disbelieved. When he was close to death, Jesus cried out, *"My God, my God, why have You forsaken me?"* this was prophesied in Psalm 22:1. Finally, Psalm 16:10 says, *"For You will not abandon my soul to Sheol; Nor will You allow Your Holy One to undergo decay."* He was bodily resurrected three days after his crucifixion; hundreds of his followers witnessed the event, this is the event that spawned the Christian movement to become the world's biggest religion. If we believe that these prophecies were fulfilled at Jesus' first appearance came to be, it will seem logical that the predictions of the second coming would also be fulfilled.

There are many verses of the Bible regarding Jesus that were partially completed. We would expect the rest of the passages to be completed on His return. For example, in Isaiah 9:6, *"For a child will be born to us, a son will be given to us; And the government will rest on His shoulders";* Jesus was born 2000 years ago but the government did not rest on his shoulders at his first coming. On the contrary, he was scorned and crucified like a common criminal. Either God lied in His word (the one thing God cannot do is lie), or this last part is still to be fulfilled. When? On Jesus' return, when He will rule the world. This is just one example of a partially fulfilled prophecy. Jesus also mentioned His second coming. Matthew 25:31, *"But when the Son of Man comes in His glory, and all the angels with Him, then He will sit on His glorious throne. All the nations will be gathered before Him; and He will separate them from one another, as the shepherd separates the sheep from the goats; and He will put the sheep on His right, and the goats on the left."* The first time Jesus came, this event never happened, so must be alluding to some future event.

The second coming of Jesus will be vastly different from the first. He came the first time in humility, born in a stable and died on the cross as a common criminal. The second coming will be "with power and great glory." On this day, in a triumphant return, the whole world will see and know who Jesus is. Humility was central in Jesus' first coming; power and glory will be apparent in His second. The second coming should not be a source of fear for a Christian if we are truly saved. It should be an event that will end the current human rule to be replaced by God's rule, so we should look forward to it.

When should we expect the second coming? During the turn of the first millennium, many supposed that Jesus was about to return. Countless rich sold all they had, giving their money to the poor and waited for the return of Christ. It never happened. They should not have been surprised as the second coming of Christ is to be preceded by the temple's rebuilding. The Jews were dispersed throughout the world, and the temple destroyed in AD 70, as predicted by Jesus in Matthew 24:1-2. The Jews had been stateless until 1948 when they returned to their homeland, and the state of Israel was formed. Never had a dispersed people managed to retain their identity through twenty centuries and re-establish their nationhood in their original land, despite anti-Semitic sentiments. We should expect the temple's rebuilding to take place before the second coming as predicted by John, Paul, and Jesus himself. Currently, seven different groups are pushing for the reconstruction of the temple in Israel. In Matthew 24:5-8, Jesus said, *"For many will come in My name, saying, 'I am the Christ,' and they will mislead many people. And you will be hearing of wars and rumours of wars. See that you are not alarmed, for those things must take place, but that is not yet the end. For nation will rise against nation, and kingdom against kingdom, and there will be famines and earthquakes in various places. But all these things are merely the beginning of birth pains.*" Finally, Jesus says to be ready for the final days, "*Therefore be on the alert, for you do not know which day your Lord is coming. But be sure of this, that if the head of the house had known at what time of the night the thief was coming, he would have been on the alert and would not have allowed his house to be broken into. For this reason you must be ready as well; for the Son of Man is coming at an hour when you do not think.*" Matthew 24:42-44.

CHAPTER 6
SUFFERING

"The truth that many people never understand, until it is too late, is that the more you try to avoid suffering the more you suffer because smaller and more insignificant things begin to torture you in proportion to your fear of being hurt."
Thomas Merton

"God brings men into deep waters not to drown them, but to cleanse them."
James H. Aughey

"God had one son on earth without sin, but never one without suffering."
Augustine

Why is there suffering?

John 16:33, "In the world you have tribulation, but take courage; I have overcome the world"

"It is the fire of suffering that brings forth the gold of godliness."

Jeanne Marie Bouvier de la Motte Guyon

Suffering! The atheist's nuclear bomb! Atheist's use suffering as an argument against God's existence as they reason, if God is all-powerful, he could and should stop suffering. This reasoning makes for an excellent argument that deserves an answer. However, it is not just the Christian that needs to answer the question of suffering. All worldviews need to explain the pain, heartache and anguish that suffering brings. What is Islam's perspective on the subject? Islam is fatalistic. The Muslim cries out, INSHALLAH, it is Gods will. Everything that happens is deterministic. Good and evil exist in the world, and that is Gods will. Buddhism maintains that good and evil do not exist. Everything is an illusion, so the Buddhist's answer is you need to detach yourself from the world. This is achieved by removing the desires and wants of this world through the seven-fold enlightenment, and essentially the question itself is an illusion. Atheism's answer is that the world has come from mindless chance, and fundamentally, the strong survive at the expense of the weak. Where we see suffering, we expect it, but there is no reason for it. Morality has no transcendent source (God). Our morality comes from our personal preferences or dictated by society. The problem is if two societies or people have different views, then there is friction. During the Nuremberg trials, the Nazis said they were "following orders" as a defence for the atrocities that they carried out. In the society the Nazis had carved out for themselves, they believed it was right and proper to follow the path they did to achieve their goals. They were killing the disabled and the ethnically undesirable. If atheism is correct, everything is purposeless. Richard Dawkins, the famous new age atheist, would have us believe that there is no good and evil. DNA is responsible for our actions and *"we dance to its music"* as he would say. If Dawkins is right, why do we care when someone we have never met suffers? There must be a reason we have compassion when we see misery. It is hard not to feel for parents that bury a child, for a mother to receive the devastating news that her baby has leukaemia. To watch a loved one die slowly of cancer. To see a parent's character slowly dwindle as brain degeneration takes the sparkle out of their eyes. On a personal note, to watch my mother suffer for 73 days in a hospital intensive care unit before eventually dying.

What is the Christian view of suffering? Can the God of the Bible put an end to suffering? If so, why does he not do so? As mentioned before, Epicurus said, *"Is God willing to prevent evil, but not able? Then he is not omnipotent. Is he able, but not willing? Then he is malevolent. Is he both able and willing? Then whence cometh evil? Is he neither able nor willing? Then why call him God?"* Can we as finite beings understand why we suffer? Can our limited minds comprehend the infinite thoughts of God and why we endure the distress of suffering? Isaiah 55:9, God proclaims, *"For as the heavens are higher than the earth, so are My ways higher than your ways, And My thoughts than your thoughts."* As an example of this disparity of understanding, I remember taking my daughter for a vaccination when she was a baby. I held her tight in my arms, bracing her (and me) for what was to come. The nurse administered the injection. My daughter let out an almighty scream as she experienced the full pain of the needle. I will never forget the look my daughter gave me as she stared at me, wide-eyed as if to say, "How could you let them hurt me?" As if to add salt into the wound, my daughter saw me thanking the nurse. As a child with her limited knowledge, my daughter could not understand why I would let her suffer like that. As a loving father, I knew the injection was to prevent worse pain if she caught a disease. Pain is bearable if you know there is a purpose in enduring it. We will put our loved ones through suffering if we know there is a greater good.

C.S. Lewis once mused, if you throw a stick at someone to hurt them, could God turn the stick into grass to avoid injuring them? If God is all-powerful, he could. However, that would take away the perpetrator's freedom of choice. People are happy for God to intervene in extreme cases like rape, murder, or the holocaust. What about the choices we all make? Such as going out for an expensive meal rather than spending the money on helping someone who is dying of starvation? God could intervene in all our decisions. However, we would be indignant at God if we were to sit down to a luxurious meal only to find the food transported to a starving person. It is our choice to love ourselves rather than our neighbour. Countless people have died from starvation that could have been saved if only "good people" would donate the money they spent on their indulgences. How painful and slow must it be to die from starvation while we in the west watch more adverts about food and dream of dining at Michelin star restaurants.

Could an all-powerful God stop suffering? There are three possibilities. Either God does not have the power to stop suffering. God allows suffering because he is not loving. Or finally, the world that God created is the only one that allows love. God could have made a world where people could only do good. That world would not allow the possibility to be loving and to love. For love to be real, it must be a choice. You cannot force someone to love you. The opposite of love is hate; you have an option to love or hate your neighbour. The Christian life is to love your neighbour as yourself. Loving your neighbour is second only to loving God. Even Hollywood understands the principle that love must be a free-will choice and not forced. In Disney's Aladdin, the "all-powerful" Genie has limits to his power. He cannot make princess Jasmine fall in love with Aladdin. In the film Bruce Almighty, god (Morgan Freeman) tells Bruce when he makes him god temporarily (a ridiculous plotline

CHAPTER 7
WHAT IS IT ALL ABOUT?

*"No matter how just your words may be, when you speak with anger,
you ruin all: no matter how boldly you speak, how fairly reprove."*
John Chrysostom

*"The Bible will keep you from sin, or sin
will keep you from the Bible."*
Dwight L. Moody

*"If to be feelingly alive to the sufferings of my fellow-
creatures is to be a fanatic, I am one of the most
incurable fanatics ever permitted to be at large."*
William Wilberforce.

Conclusion

Psalm 31:24 "Be strong and let your heart take courage, All you who wait for the LORD."

> *"Good intentions and earnest effort are not enough.*
> *Only Jesus can make an otherwise futile life productive."*
> *Chuck Swindoll*

The truth is out there

The truth about life and love boils down to this simple equation. Either there is a God who created everything or there is not and life as we know it is the result of some random cosmic accident. I find myself at odds with the prominent thinkers of the twenty-first century who believe the later. Stephen Hawking would have us believe that the universe comes from "nothing." Armed with my prised qualification, my 100 yards swimming certificate, I have the audacity to disagree.

The view being taught in our schools today is that we are here by accident based on, as I have tried to demonstrate, unproven scientific theories. Which of these two views a person holds will profoundly affect how humankind interact with each other? If we think that we are all the result of some random DNA mutations, then there is no intrinsic purpose to life. We all invent our own purpose; some will make money their purpose, others power and yet others sexual relationships. The problem with these human-made purposes to life is that they will inevitably conflict with another's purpose. Inescapably, this will lead to the rise in tensions that we see in society today. The rich are getting richer at the expense of the poor. I read somewhere that the eight richest people in the world have the same wealth as the poorest half of the world's population. Mental illness is on the increase. Famine is prevalent. Wars and rumours of wars are beamed to our TV screens constantly, fulfilling Bible prophecies, *"Behold, Damascus is about to be removed from being a city and will become a fallen ruin."* Isaiah 17:1. Men struggle to form relationships with women because pornography is so prevalent. Men see the instant gratification that occurs in these short films (the average "relationship" last 9 minutes), and struggle to understand why reality is not the same. This leads to the increase in sexual violence as men emulate what they think is "normal" behaviour from what they see in pornography.

On the flip side, if we believe that we are all creatures of God, created by God for a purpose on purpose and everyone's life is sacred and of infinite value. That understanding will mean respect for your fellow man and believe that God's laws enshrine those rights.

In the final analysis, this book's title seemed so all-encompassing and too big a claim, that is, "Finding Truth in Life and Love: One Man's Journey." In fact, it is not big or bold enough to answer every question a person has in such a small book. To be honest little of this material is purely my thoughts. You only need to look at how much of this material is in *italics* to realise that (there are over two hundred quotes). Many infinitely greater minds than mine have influenced me. Investigators like Jim Wallace and Lee Strobel set out to prove Christianity false but became Christians when faced with the historical evidence. C. S. Lewis, an atheist who said on his conversion that he was the most reluctant convert in England. Nabeel Qureshi and Abu Murray, both Muslims who made the difficult transition to Christianity, costing them fellowship with their family. These are just some of the people who helped me on my journey, culminated in my current worldview. Oddly enough, many non-believers have also helped me in my voyage of discovery. Christopher Hitchens (RIP), one of the most outstanding debaters I have ever heard, argued the case for atheism in his typically charismatic, persuasive way. Still, Christopher Hitchens offered no purpose and no hope that came with his views, and most importantly, he could not disprove God's existence despite passionate and sometimes abrasive efforts on his part. The same can be said for Richard Dawkins, who believes there is *"no purpose, no evil, no good, nothing but blind, pitiless indifference."* My religious education teacher tried to explain away miracles as natural phenomena enraged me; I am not quite sure why as I did not believe the Bible was the inspired word of God at the time. I hope I have made the case that belief in God is logical and that He is knowable through the Bible's pages. The Bible tells us how the world started (origin), where this mortal body will end up (destiny). How between these two events, we are to live our lives (morality) and why we are here (meaning).

This book's purpose is to give a defence of the worldview that I believe is the most rational and makes sense of a lost world. I would never have believed that this ancient religion would make so much sense logically speaking at the start of my journey. As Christians, we need to *"always being ready to make a defence to everyone who asks you to give an account for the hope that is in you, yet with gentleness and reverence." 1 Peter 3:15.* John Chrysostom said, *"There is nothing colder than a Christian who does not seek to save others."*

I am sure people will read this book and say the authors a fraud, he makes himself so holy and pious, but I heard he was less than exemplary on this occasion and on that. And you should see him when he loses his temper; it is quite shocking. To that, I say, you do not know the half of it. And that is just the bad stuff that I know I am doing wrong. I do not doubt that there are numerous occasions when I have not been loving, not noticing those close to me needed a hug or a kind word when they were suffering, overlooked because I have been so wrapped up in my own life to notice. Not to mention all the needy in the world that I could help if only I did not spend money on pointless endeavours and things I do not really need. Thankfully, Christianity does not depend on me and my good works. No, unlike other religions, the central theme of Christianity is you cannot be worthy in your own right. We need someone to save us, and that must be a perfect person. That person is, of course, Jesus. If we could be faultless and earn our way to His presence, then there would be no need for the cross. Until we understand that we will never be good enough on our own merit, and so need to be literally eternally grateful for the one that justifies us. I saw a bumper sticker once, which summed it up quite nicely. It read, *"Christians are not perfect, but they are saved."* Churches are not full of righteous people but people who know they are spiritually sick and need healing.

Predestination – a barrier to belief?

How is it that identical twins, brought up in the same way with virtually identical genetics, but one becomes a Christian and the other an atheist? An example of this is two famous brothers (admittedly not identical twins), Christopher Hitchens (RIP), a new age atheist and his brother, Peter Hitchens, a Christian. Their disagreements on theological issues were very stark. Peter touches on this in his book *"The Rage against God."* How do these diametrically opposed views come to be when you would expect nurture and nature to have a similar effect on the brothers? I wish I could answer that for certainty, but I believe it has to do with having our names written in the book of life. The Bible tells us, *"He chose us in Him before the foundation of the world."* Ephesians 1:4. Again, *"You did not choose Me but I chose you,"* John 15:16. It sounds like predestination, the great debate of countless philosophers. That is, are we predisposed to doing something based on our genes and our upbringing, as well as the influence the environment has on us or do we have free will? The late Steven Hawking said that if you could know everything there is to know in the universe (inadvertently inventing God), how every atom would interact with every other, you would know exactly how everyone would respond in every situation. You would know if person A would turn left while person B would turn right in any given situation. A somewhat poor example of this is my wife loves shoes. I can predict without fail that she cannot walk past a shoe shop without looking inside. I know this because I know my wife and can tell what she will do when faced with a shoe shop's temptation. I am not a philosopher, but I think the answer has already been given inadvertently by Steven Hawking, that is, God is all-knowing and outside the created concept of time. So yesterday, today, and tomorrow are all the same to God. Therefore, He knows whose name is to be entered into the book of life before time plays out as he knows us *"Before I formed you in the womb I knew you,"* Jeremiah 1:5. This concept may be hard to grasp, I admit and even harder to write. I feel an extended coffee break and a lie down coming on, but it does, at least in my mind, explain the puzzle of who is chosen to be followers of Christ.

Miracles and pain

Is there enough evidence in the Bible and the world around us to believe in a creator God? Well, you cannot prove God the same way as you can prove gravity. God is outside the laws of physics, so it would seem logical that you could not use the laws within physics to explain something outside of science. Having a conversation with a relative of mine, he said that he did not believe in anything supernatural and by extension the Bible because he is an engineer. This made me chuckle as being an engineer myself is exactly why I believe the Bible account of creation. Things do not happen without a cause, regardless of what some of the great thinkers would have us believe.

Supernatural events like miracles are often cited as the main stumbling block for people not believing in God. We do not experience young girls becoming pregnant without a partner, the blind do not start to see, and indeed the dead do not come alive. Could a God outside the laws of science intervene in these laws, suspending them to perform miraculous acts? There could be several individual explanations for some of the wonders we see in the universe. How the universe is so delicately balanced, how life started from lifelessness, but one explanation covers them all. That is, God created the universe, the earth, you, and me on purpose and for a purpose. If you believe this, everything is easier to bear, even pain.

Pain is hard to endure if there is no purpose behind it, but you will bear the dentist's drill to alleviate a toothache. You would be surprised how much pain you can tolerate. I remember suffering from toothache for years. I saw numerous dentists, but the pain persisted. While on holiday in Cyprus, my mother insisted that I see a dentist. This guy was the Cyprus dentist association's answer to Clint Eastwood. He investigated my tooth with a cigarette dangling from his lips and declared he could fix the toothache. He started to drill away. I was sweating profusely. He stopped and looked at me and asked if I was scared? I replied no, I was just in a lot of pain. But I was happy to endure the pain for a short while to alleviate the suffering long term. By the way, the cowboy dentist did manage to sort out my toothache where others had failed.

A final word

You may say the price of Christianity is too high, the guy is a Christian nut job, and besides, I do not believe any of this. If you are lucky and Christianity is not true, that is, we come from nothing and go to nothing. Eventually, entropy will win. The body will breakdown and stop working. We will become part of the ultimate statistic, which is 10 out of 10 die. We will all end up with a tombstone with two dates on it, one for our birth and one for our death, with a dash separating the two events. In years to come people will wonder what good and what use you put your dash to while they divide up your wealth. If you are unlucky and Christianity is true, but you have not given your life to Christ. In that case, justice demands that the non-believers will be separated from the believers, the lambs from the goats, Matthew 25:31, the wheat from the chaff, spending eternity living in regret. Are you sure you want to take that chance and put Christ aside?

You may ask, even if Christianity is real, how does it help me live my life in an increasingly hostile world? As I mentioned in the first few pages of this book, I inherited many of my mother's traits. She had so many phobias and was a born worrier. I remember saying to my mum on one occasion why was she worried? She replied she was worried because *"there was nothing to worry about."* The point is that she always expected her life to be full of woes, and when there was nothing particularly troubling at that time, she was disturbed, expecting some tragedy or other to befall her any minute. One of the practical benefits of being a Christian is that these phobias and worries are not quite as life-limiting as before. I remember a specific occasion in 2014 when the bottom fell out of my life. While sparing you the details, I would cry for no reason, struggling to cope with the seemingly mountainous issues in my life. I saw my doctor, who diagnosed me as being clinically depressed and prescribed a course of antidepressants. I remember looking at these tablets, thinking that they would help ease the pain, the anxiety, and the struggles I was facing. On the flip side, I know that these drugs have side effects and can lead to dependency. While I measured up the pros and cons, I suddenly remembered a passage from 1 Corinthians 10:13, *"God is faithful, so He will not allow you to be tempted beyond what you are able, but with the temptation will provide the way of escape also, so that you will be able to endure it."* I thought to myself, I might as well find out if this is true sooner rather than later, so tossed the tablets aside. True to scripture, I was able to endure the difficulties in my life at the time. So, while I have not completely overcome all my inherited shortcomings, they are certainly less prevalent in my life. The words of Corrie Ten Boom sums this up brilliantly, *"Worry does not empty tomorrow of its sorrows; it empties today of its strength."*

Some may be tempted to follow the example of that great philosopher of the 20th century. I am, off course referring to Bart Simpson from the TV show "The Simpsons." Barts philosophy is to *"go for the life of sin, followed by the presto-change-o deathbed repentance."* I think waiting for a death bed change of life is a poor strategy indeed and will end up with eternal consequences that you will regret. There is only one winner when playing dice with God.

A word of warning. If you are moved to explore the Christian life, it will cost you. It will cost you your time because you will want to do God's will rather than your will. It will cost you money because you will want to spend your money on what God wants rather than what you want. The first place in your heart will no longer be you and your loved ones but reserved for God. That is not to say you will no longer love your family. On the contrary, you will love them more because you will be aware that they are gifts from God, made in His image, and so to be cherished.

I hope that all whom started this book have continued through the pages to this point. I suspect that some may have stopped reading after the first few pages thinking, "The author's right, this book will never be a best-seller," tossing the book aside. Being a best-seller was never my motivation. If only one person reads this book and says, the writer has a point, let me investigate for myself his outrageous claims that God became man and died for His creation, it would have been worth the countless hours of reading, research, and writing. As mentioned previously, I am no literary expert so every word, every sentence, every paragraph, and every chapter are difficult for me to express and needs to be amended thanks to the magic of Microsoft Word and some wonderful friends and family that have helped with the literary review. If only I paid more attention in English classes!

One final point. In John 18:37-38, there is an exchange of words between Jesus and Pilot. *Jesus answered, "You say correctly that I am a king. For this purpose I have been born, and for this I have come into the world: to testify to the truth. Everyone who is of the truth listens to My voice." Pilot said to Him, "What is truth?"* Pilot never waited to hear the answer and walked away from the one person, Jesus, that knew the truth. Will you do the same?

Thank you for taking the time to read this book. I truly hope and pray that you will be inspired to take the next steps on your own journey to discovering the truth about Life and Love.

"Belief is a wise wager. Granted that faith cannot be proved, what harm will come to you if you gamble on its truth and it proves false? If you gain, you gain all; if you lose, you lose nothing. Wager, then, without hesitation, that He exists."
Blaise Pascal

"The dirtier your Bible, the cleaner your heart!"
Victor Manuel Rivera

"I tell you, there is joy in the presence of the angels of God over one sinner who repents."
Luke 15:10

"God never said that the journey would be easy, but He did say that the arrival would be worthwhile."
Max Lucado

"And I say to you, Ask, and it shall be given you; seek, and ye shall find; knock, and it shall be opened to you. For every one that asketh receiveth; and he that seeketh findeth, and to him that knocketh it shall be opened."
Luke 11:9-10

BIBLIOGRAPHY

A E Wilder-Smith, *"The Natural Sciences Know Nothing of Evolution"*
Jim Wallace, *"Cold Case Christianity"*
Lee Strobel, *"The Case for Christ"*
Nabeel Qureshi, *"Seeking Allah finding Jesus"*
Peter Hitchens, *"The Rage Against God"*
Stephen Meyers, *"Darwin's Doubt"*

Books recommended by the author
Abdu H. Murray, *"Grand Central Question"*
Abdu H. Murray, *"Saving Truth"*
Amy Orr-Ewing, *"Where is God in All the Suffering"*
Antony Flew, *"There Is a God"*
C.S. Lewis, *"Mere Christianity"*
Charles H. Spurgeon, *"Jesus Came to Save Sinners"*
Charles Swindoll, *"Searching the Scriptures"*
Christine Cane, *"Unexpected"*
Christine Cane, *"Unashamed"*
Chuck Missler, *"Learn the Bible in 24 Hours"*
Chuck Missler, *"The book of Genesis: An Expositional Commentary"*

Corrier Ten Boon, "The hiding Place"

David Berlinski "The Devil's Delusion"

Frank Morison, "Who moved the stone"

James L. Snyder "No Greater Love"

Jim Wallace, "Person of Interest"

John Bunyan, "The Pilgrims Progress"

John Lennox, "Against the Flow"

John Lennox, "God's undertaker"

John MacArthur, "The Inerrant word"

John R. W. Stott, "The Cross of Christ"

Josh and Sean McDowell, "Evidence that Demand a Verdict"

Nabeel Qureshi, "No God but one: Allah or Jesus?"

R C Sproul "Foundations"

Ravi Zacharias, "Has Christianity Failed You"

Ravi Zacharias, "The Logic of God"

Rick Warren, "The Purpose Driven Life"

Stephen Mansfield, "Killing Jesus"

Thomas A Kempas "The Imitation of Christ"

Timothy Keller, "The reason for God"

Yiayia Eleni
By Theodosis Kyriacou

From the heat of Cyprus
Out in the cold and wet of England
Freezing her toes and fingers
Frying fish and cutting potatoes.

My yiayia **Eleni**
When family was the world to you
When untied a sense of completeness,
We have learnt the importance of nearness
This I tell you is true.

Your long, tight embraces
Your slobbering sloppy kisses,
The beckon of a name
The closeness of your frame.

My yiayia **Eleni**
When you cook, you serve a feast
Always with love but a dash of inelegance!

Kleftiko
Lamb and potatoes
Stews and
Soups

'Eat', 'eat'
You don't eat enough
But don't eat too much or you'll becomes 'fats'.
Never enough
But never too much,

'Go on put some more'
Sweep the floor
And 'keys the door'

A superstitious one
You bless every corner of the house by blanketing Incense
Your fear and reverence
For God and the Saints
Teaches us to live a life as miraculous as yours.

But we remember you more than the laughs,
the big food and the big family.
It was your big love
That you taught us so unconditionally.

My yiayia **Eleni**
A great mother
A great wife,
A yiayia like no other
We can't wait to see you in the new life

My yiayia **Eleni**
Our yiayia **Eleni**

ABOUT THE AUTHOR

The author has been an engineer for most of his working life. As an engineer, logic has been the bedrock of his career which has helped him build and maintain all kinds of broadcast systems. This logical approach to engineering has gained him a well-respected reputation within his field. When the author applies the same analytical approach to life, it has led him on an epic journey of discovery. He has been fascinated with history and origins from a young age, always prepared to challenge what others have said if it does not seem to cohere with logic and common sense. As a nominal Christian from birth, he often wondered why he was a "Christian". If he was born into a Muslim family, would he be a Muslim? The religion a person is born into seems to be a poor reason to follow any belief system. The only qualification any faith system would need to make it worth following is if that system is true. The author embarked on a lifelong journey for truth. He has noticed the lack of logic applied to everyday life. The world has become increasingly confusing where the truth has been the casualty of political correctness. The author has written his first book, "Finding Truth in Life and Love: One Man's Journey", to help explain his view of life from what seems to be the most logical view of the world and how to live life. That is the view from a Christian world perspective.

Printed in the United States
by Baker & Taylor Publisher Services